# What People Are Saying About
## *How to Be Like Mike* . . .

"Pat Williams is a great motivational speaker, and now motivates us again using the life and characteristics of Michael Jordan. Pat has captured much of what makes Michael, Michael, and in doing so will help you reach your potential."

—**Dean Smith**
former head basketball coach, University of North Carolina

"Pat Williams writes the book that could be a collaboration of Dale Carnegie and Studs Terkel. He talks to everyday people about the most unique person. And he comes away with a guide to success."

—**Sam Smith**
sportswriter, *Chicago Tribune*

"*How to Be Like Mike* is an insight into the tools that made Michael Jordan the best competitor in sports. In order to win, you have to hate losing, and nobody loathed that feeling more than Michael. He possessed a unique ability to turn any task into competition and the uncompromising will to win any battle. Someone may come along with comparable athletic skills, but what set Michael apart was his mental strength."

—**George Karl**
NBA head coach

"Be it sports, politics or life, Pat Williams shows us how to get it done—the Michael Jordan way."

—**Tim Russert**
moderator, NBC's *Meet the Press*

"Fascinating and entertaining! Learn and relive the success secrets from the most amazing basketball player by the most amazing storyteller. Great stuff!"

—**Pat Croce**
former president, Philadelphia 76ers

"The coaching profession is a very competitive one where everybody's always looking to get better. As long as you weren't coaching against him, Michael Jordan was an absolute joy to watch. Pat Williams's new book was an absolute joy to read. And you'll be a better coach and person after you've read it."

—**Jerry Tarkanian**
head basketball coach, Fresno State University

"This is Pat Williams's best book yet. Anyone who reads this will never again ask, 'Why was Michael Jordan so special?' Young and old alike will be inspired to excellence after reading *How to Be Like Mike*."

—**Bill Fitch**
former NBA coach

"Inspiration begets inspiration! Hundreds of wonderful stories accounting the personal experiences by those people closest to Michael Jordan. You'll learn about Mike from those who truly knew him best!"

—**John Gabriel**
general manager, Orlando Magic

"Pat Williams demonstrates he is both an observant student and astute teacher when describing the natural relationship that exists between athletic competition and inspirational messages. While none of us will ever truly know what special ingredients make Michael Jordan the competitor he is, *How to Be Like Mike* comes as close to capturing the essence of Mr. Jordan as I've seen while providing inspiration to us all."

—**Kevin Johnson**
former NBA player

"This book is filled with priceless information way beyond Michael Jordan. Do yourself a favor—read it and then buy a copy for everyone in your galaxy."

—**Lefty Driesell**
longtime college basketball coach

"I'm assigning *How to Be Like Mike* as required reading for my players at the University of Louisville. This is a terrific book that is going to have wide-ranging impact."

—**Rick Pitino**
head basketball coach, University of Louisville

"Pat Williams has done it again! No one can capture the great qualities of Michael Jordan like Pat. This is a 'must read' for anyone associated with sports."

—**Lute Olson**
head basketball coach, University of Arizona

"Pat Williams has done a thorough research job on this book and now we all know what has to be done to be like Mike. I couldn't stop reading."

—**Doc Rivers**
head coach, Orlando Magic

To Charlie —
Win!

*[signature]*

# How to Be Like
# MIKE

## LIFE LESSONS ABOUT BASKETBALL'S BEST

## Pat Williams
## With Michael Weinreb

Health Communications, Inc.
Deerfield Beach, Florida

*www.bcibooks.com*

**Library of Congress Cataloging-in-Publication Data**
**is available through the Library of Congress.**

© 2001 Pat Williams

ISBN-13: 978-1-55874-955-9 (trade paper)
ISBN-10: 1-55874-955-1 (trade paper)

Publisher: Health Communications, Inc.
3201 S.W. 15th Street
Deerfield Beach, FL 33442-8190

R-01-07

*Cover design by Lisa Camp*
*Cover photo by ALLSPORT Photography*
*Inside book design by Lawna Patterson Oldfield*

**Pat Williams:**
To my son Michael—
May the lessons of this "other"
Michael penetrate your life.

**Michael Weinreb:**
To my grandmothers, B and E,
who have probably never heard
of this "other" Michael.

# Other Books by Pat Williams

The Gingerbread Man

The Power Within You

We Owed You One

Nothing but Winners

Rekindled

Keep the Fire Glowing

Just Between Us

Twelve Part Harmony

Kindling

Love Her, Like Him

Making Magic

Jock Jokes

Go for the Magic

The Magic of Teamwork

Ahead of the Game

A Lifetime of Success

Marketing Your Dreams

Secrets from the Mountain

It Happens on Sunday

# CONTENTS

# ACKNOWLEDGMENTS

I would like to thank Bob Vander Weide, president and CEO of RDV Sports, and the RDV Sports family; Melinda Ethington, my invaluable assistant; Leslie Boucher and Hank Martens of the mailroom at RDV Sports; Ken Hussar and Bob Rosenberg for their thorough proofreading of this book; Mark Victor Hansen, for his encouragement; Peter Vegso of Health Communications, Inc., and his fine staff, including Christine Belleris, Allison Janse, Lisa Drucker, Susan Tobias, Larissa Hise Henoch, Lawna Patterson Oldfield, Dawn Grove, Anthony Clausi, Terry Burke, Kim Weiss and Kelly Maragni; to Bryan Harris, book promoter extraordinaire; Michael Weinreb, a skilled young writer who has organized this material brilliantly; my wife, Ruth, and our children, who have been so supportive of this project.

—Pat Williams

Thanks to Steve, Nancy, Paul, Carolyn, Adam and Alexander Weinreb; to my friends, especially Kevin Gorman, Damian Dobrosielski, B. J. Reyes, Ryan Jones, Chuck Klosterman, David Giffels, Beth McNichol, Greg Couch and Steve Recker; to Terry Pluto, Larry Pantages, the memory of Jim Derendal and all of my colleagues and friends in Akron; and to all of my classmates in the Boston University fiction writing program. And thanks, of course, to Pat Williams, for his unceasing energy, and for his belief in both the project and in me.

David Halberstam's biography of Jordan, *Playing for Keeps,* was a wonderful resource and inspiration.

—Michael Weinreb

# JUST FOR TEENS: MIKE IN THE MIRROR

Congratulations! As a teenager, you have made a wise choice in selecting this book. Your second great decision is to aspire to be like Mike. Surely be yourself (nobody else wants the job), but as you assimilate Michael's traits and begin to release those Jordan endorphins, you will have a major head start on your peers. (As one who has raised nineteen teenagers and has interviewed over 1,500 people about Michael Jordan, some might consider me an authority on both subjects.) Attach this handy checklist to your mirror so you will be able to take a daily progress inventory of your mission to be like Mike.

☑ **Focus.** Train your mind to concentrate upon the essentials and discard the frivolous and unimportant.

☑ **Passion & Energy.** Enthusiasm is one of the greatest emotions. Without it there is no achievement. With it, a new idea can win over an old idea.

☑ **Hard Work.** If you want to leave your footprints on the sands of time, you'd better wear work shoes.

☑ **Perseverance.** Perseverance is not a long race; it is many short races one after another.

☑ **Responsibility.** "Success on any major scale requires you to accept responsibility. . . . In the final analysis, the one quality that all successful people have is the ability to take on responsibility."

—Michael Korda

☑ **Influence.** The greatest of motivational principles is: People do what people see. As adults we are still playing Follow the Leader.

☑ **Competing and Winning.** Winners expect to win in advance. Life is a self-fulfilling prophecy.

☑ **Teamwork.** People support what they help create.

☑ **Leadership.** Good leadership should do more than attract followers. It should produce more leaders.

☑ **Respect, Trust, Loyalty.** There's only one thing finer than a friend you can trust, and that's one who trusts you.

☑ **Character.** We all want character, but not the trials that produce it. You can't build character in a cocoon.

—Pat Williams

# FOREWORD

## By Grant Hill
## Orlando Magic All-Star

Even though tens of thousands wear Air Jordans, there will never be another who fills Michael Jordan's shoes—and I know from personal experience! I am flattered by comparisons, but realistically I can never live up to his achievements. What MJ has done for basketball, sports in general, race relations ... it's incalculable. It's time to give "Who's going to be the next Michael Jordan?" a rest. It's unfair to Michael and to every other aspiring athlete.

The fascination with MJ continues. Will he return? People want him back so badly. He has had such an enormous hold on us and our culture. His presence as an active player has been sorely missed.

The eleven chapters that follow capture Michael's persona perfectly. He schooled us on and off the court, and as one of his students, I give him A pluses across the board.

→ **Focus.** With a game on the line, MJ could achieve a level of focus no one else could reach. He never got rattled. His concentration was impenetrable. It was part of his genius.

→ **Passion & Energy.** Michael is passionate about basketball and truly loved playing. His energy level allowed him to overcome fatigue in a remarkable, transcendent way.

→ **Work.** Difficult as it is to recall, MJ did have weaknesses when he entered the NBA, but he worked tirelessly to improve and soon those weaknesses—defense and outside shooting— became his added strengths.

→ **Perseverance.** MJ won through his will. He was such a tough opponent because he would never quit. I can speak firsthand as to how frustrating that is to an opponent!

→ **Responsibility.** MJ lives—and thrives—under a microscope. I believe this visibility intensifies his sense of responsibility to his sport, family, community and country.

→ **Influence.** What an influence and impact MJ has been to millions—not simply to the wannabes on the playgrounds—but to us in the NBA, too. Tracy McGrady, Shaq, Kobe, Allen Iverson and I are still striving to emulate him—yes, to be like Mike! He is truly the role model's role model. He personifies how to conduct oneself on and off the court.

→ **Competing and Winning.** I believe his competitive juices boil. It is known far and wide that MJ hates to lose, be it a simple card game or a Game Seven in the Finals. He always wants to win and that championship passion fuels him.

→ **Teamwork.** MJ is the ultimate one-on-one player, yet he understands that winning big is determined by involving his teammates. Putting that philosophy in sneakers daily translated into a dynasty of six titles in eight years.

→ **Leadership.** MJ leads by example. He demands no more from his teammates than he demands from himself.

→ **Respect, Trust, Loyalty.** Michael has a great respect for the game and the people in the game, and he reveres his predecessors who provided the foundation for today's NBA. When you respect people, they trust you, and trust breeds loyalty. For example, the loyalty MJ had for coach Phil Jackson is rare in our profession.

➔ **Character.** Michael is certainly not perfect. He is flawed like the rest of us. It is obvious to those of us who know him well, and probably to even casual observers, that quality of character has been embedded in his make-up. How else can one explain his self-discipline, humility, honesty, integrity and courage?

Pat Williams and Michael Weinreb have captured the essence of Michael Jordan in an extraordinary way. This book is thoroughly researched, and the lessons from MJ's career are so vividly explained that you will be able to apply them in your life. When you have "completed the MJ course," you will discover that all of us can be like Mike.

*August 1, 2001*
*Orlando, Florida*

# WORD OF TRIBUTE

## By Doug Collins
## Head Coach, Washington Wizards

Anyone who knows Michael Jordan and is asked to comment about him runs the risk of running out of superlatives but is never in danger of being accused of hyperbole. My first head coaching job in the NBA was with the Chicago Bulls, and I had the privilege of coaching Michael early in his pro career.

Not only is Michael a coach's dream, but he's a sportswriter's/commentator's godsend because in reporting on his achievements on and off the court, it takes little time to compose a litany of praise.

When reflecting on MJ, these words immediately come to mind . . .

- ultimate competitor
- quintessential example

- punctual
- prepared
- respectful

Michael brought his "A game" every night, no matter who the competition was. Before each game I would observe him dealing with the media and his legions of fans, and then, as if an alarm would sound in his head, his focus would shift, and you could read in his eyes, "I'm ready for combat."

He would bring that same intensity to practice and win every sprint. He was always punctual, and he set an example for his teammates by working hard daily. His professionalism and leadership meant that I didn't have to say a whole lot to get the players motivated. His inner fire served to spark his teammates to perform at their highest level.

Michael was the most fundamentally sound player I have ever seen. Rick Majerus, head coach at the University of Utah, would show his players a highlight film of what things Jordan, the ultimate player, would do on the court. The highlights contained no footage of Michael posterizing an opponent with a thunderous dunk or a dazzling, gravity-defying pirouette on the way to the bucket. What the tape did show, however, was Michael dishing assists, filling the lane, playing defense, diving after loose balls, taking charges. . . .

In my basketball career I have been associated with many great players, but there is only one Michael Jordan. No one that I have witnessed has his passion for the game. He is a gym rat at heart.

In addition to his incredible skill and performance level, he has a great respect for the fans, his coaches, the competition, his fellow players and the game itself. He respects those who preceded him in elevating the level of play in the NBA, particularly Julius Erving.

To this day when I think of Michael Jordan, I get a warm feeling. He gave me the chance to be successful as a coach, and I will be forever grateful for that.

Since I left as the Bulls' coach over ten years ago, I've enjoyed watching Michael's unbelievable success from afar. During the whole period, I've wrestled with two questions: did Michael respect me as a coach, and did I help him in his career?

So, you can imagine my feelings when my phone rang in late April 2001. It was Michael, asking me for my help and telling me he wanted me to come to Washington and coach his franchise, the Wizards. That was the ultimate sign of respect to me. Here was the greatest player of all time, building a team from the ground up, and he wanted me! Wow! That's like a golfer getting a call from Tiger Woods asking him to play on his team.

Michael's call to me closed the cycle of my life and career. I felt as if I had come full circle.

Pat Williams and Michael Weinreb have done an amazing job of research in capturing the essence of Michael Jordan. When you read about the eleven attributes that characterize Michael, I can assure you that you won't become another Mike. There is only one Michael Jordan. But I can also guarantee that as you apply these characteristics to your daily regimen, you will be preparing yourself to perform at a championship level.

*August 1, 2001*
*Washington, D.C.*

# A MEMORY OF A YOUNG MICHAEL JORDAN

## By Richard Neher
## Michael's Babe Ruth League Baseball Coach

I coached Michael when he was thirteen, fourteen and fifteen years old. Michael Jordan was never an all-star when he played as a young boy. He was just a typical kid playing little league, but he was so loose and so competitive.

When Michael was thirteen, our team's fifteen-year-old catcher got hurt and we were desperate for a replacement. The rail-thin Jordan volunteered—"I'll catch, coach!"—even though it took him three bounces to throw the ball to second base. I turned down Michael's offer. He came back at me with, "Coach, if they run, I'll gun!" Even then, Michael thought he could do anything. He had that confidence.

We were playing Mutual of Omaha for first place that night and I stuck Michael back there. During infield practice, he bounced the ball to second and the other team started mocking him. Mike yelled at them, "You run, I'll gun!" Sure enough, in the second inning he threw out three straight guys trying to steal —on the bounce!

As far as basketball, Mike was just another gunner as a ten and eleven-year-old. He'd take thirty shots a game and if you passed him the ball, it wasn't coming back. In the ninth grade, he was just a 5'9" guard, that's all. Don't let anyone tell you they saw greatness back in those days.

*August 1, 2001*
*Wilmington, North Carolina*

# A MICHAEL JORDAN MEMORY

## By Harvey Araton
## Sports Columnist, *The New York Times*

My most vivid Michael Jordan memory is not one of him in the air or on the drive or celebrating the winning of another ring. It is a moment few of us outside the circle of these great athletes would ever be privileged to witness. I just got lucky. It was 1992, the Eastern Conference semifinals at Madison Square Garden, Pat Riley's Knicks trying to stay alive and going about it in their new and brutish ways. It was the second half, the Knicks asserting control. Scottie Pippen had the ball in transition and seemed to be going in for a layup when suddenly he was hog-tied by John Starks and thrown to the floor. Time-out. Pippen, dazed, even bloodied, staggered to a seat on the bench. Seated at the edge of the press table, practically on the

Bulls' bench, I had a clear look into the team's huddle, where, astonishingly enough, Jordan practically shoved Phil Jackson out of the way and kneeled right in front of his young and intimidated teammate. For about five seconds, he just stared at him, hard, and then he put his hand on Pippen's knee. "Don't you dare take that from them!" Jordan screamed. "Don't let them do that to you! You're getting the ball and you take it to the hole as hard as you can!" I will never forget the look in Jordan's eyes that night. It was as controlled a rage as I've ever seen, which I've always believed was as essential to Jordan's greatness as any part of his game. He had the ability to simultaneously balance anger and composure, regardless of the situation. If the opponent didn't provoke him, Jordan found a way to inspire himself. If I had been Pippen that night, I would have been far more afraid to disappoint Michael than I would have been of Starks, Xavier McDaniel, Anthony Mason and Charles Oakley put together.

# PROLOGUE

I am not a man who lives with a great deal of regret. But there are times, every so often, when I will spring forth from my bed in the middle of the night, hair standing in static spikes, and shake off the specter of a haunting nightmare. There are not many executives who can say they allowed the greatest athlete of the twentieth century to slide through their helpless grasp. And I'm one of them.

Allow me to explain.

I have spent my life in sports, in various front offices, in both baseball and basketball. By 1978, I was entrenched as the general manager of the NBA's Philadelphia 76ers, who were coached by Billy Cunningham. And that fall, Billy Cunningham had a problem. It involved one of his players. His name was Lloyd Free. Eventually, Lloyd would change his legal name to World B. Free, and he would hover around the pro basketball world for what seemed like an eternity, taking ridiculously long jump shots and filling eager reporters' notebooks with some of the ripest quotes they'd ever been given. He was an immense offensive talent, innovative and exciting and well-liked by the fans. It's just that Lloyd sometimes forgot that he belonged to a team. He did not believe in the utility of the pass.

So in the fall of 1978, it was my job to trade Lloyd Free. And I tried. I really did. But Lloyd's reputation preceded him. I couldn't get anything done, couldn't get anyone to risk their reputation on Lloyd. The season approached. The day before it began, I was rescued—by the Clippers, of all entities.

The Clippers were in San Diego back then. Didn't matter. They were still hapless and bumbling and ill-managed, one of the most aimless franchises in the history of organized sports. Their new coach was Gene Shue, who had coached Lloyd Free in Philadelphia, and was now willing to gamble on Lloyd.

There was a catch, of course. He was willing to gamble on Lloyd in exchange for virtually nothing. Being desperate, I took the deal. I traded Lloyd Free to the Clippers for a first-round draft pick.

That is, a first-round pick in 1984. Six years hence.

Which, in the transitional world of pro basketball, might as well have been the year 2050.

I probably don't have to tell you that the local media roasted me. They thought I'd given Lloyd away, which I denied, even though, of course, I basically had. But what did I know? Chances were it wouldn't even matter. This is a tumultuous business. Who knew where I would be in six years?

Six years later, in 1984, I was still in Philadelphia. And the Clippers were still awful. And we still had the rights to their number-one draft pick. This was before the draft lottery had originated, so the commissioner would simply flip a coin between the worst team in the Eastern Conference and the worst team in the Western Conference to determine who got the top pick. Barring some colossal reversals of fortune, the Clippers appeared destined for the coin toss.

We already knew this was a rich draft. Sam Bowie and Sam Perkins were the top seniors, and Hakeem Olajuwon and Charles Barkley were juniors who were expected to declare themselves eligible. So was a lanky guard from North Carolina whose name will figure prominently in this book.

We wcrc busy reveling in the misery of the Clippers, anticipating the coin toss, when something catastrophic occurred. Houston, the only team in the West that could challenge the Clippers for the coin-toss position, launched into a prolifically weird losing streak. I say weird because this was not the typically unwelcome nosedive. It seemed almost planned, pre-meditated, which, of course, it almost certainly was. Exhibit A: Elvin Hayes, who was then nearing senior-citizen status, played fifty-three minutes in one over-time game.

Still, on one of the final nights of the season, all we needed was for the Clippers to lose. Now, asking the Clippers to lose is not exactly a monumental request. This is a franchise that seemingly goes decades with-out winning a game.

But on this night, the Clippers won. And Houston lost. And in the end, we lost. We tumbled out of the coin toss, and the Rockets slipped in and won it and picked Olajuwon. Portland, picking second, chose Sam Bowie. We had dropped to the fifth pick, and chose Barkley. Not exactly a poor selection. But with the third pick, Chicago chose . . . well, you know who Chicago chose. Children in third-world countries know who Chicago chose. I can't even repeat it right now. I just know that seventeen years later, it still haunts my dreams.

It's easy enough to rationalize, to console myself

with the notion that it's technically not my fault, the way Houston conspired to ineptness. And that we might not have won the coin toss if we'd ever gotten that far. And that even if we had, we could have chosen any of that pool of players. And that we did get Barkley.

But Billy Cunningham was a North Carolina graduate. He had an unfettered pipeline to North Carolina Coach Dean Smith, and I don't think Dean Smith would have allowed Billy to go away without picking his player.

So I think about it. Of course I do. Michael Jordan escaped me. That's not a feeling you shake off in the span of a single lifetime.

This is fourteen years later, in 1998. I'm watching Game Six of the NBA Finals, Chicago versus Utah, and so is an overwhelming and curious segment of the world. We've begun to figure that this is it for Michael Jordan, that this is his final appearance in uniform, his glorious and final vanishing point from pro basketball. He's not saying. He's hiding behind a knowing smirk, but it's implied.

The series has been grueling. Jordan's legs are gone, but he continues to push toward the basket for lay-ups, for fouls, for free throws. There are 18.9 seconds left when Jordan skulks in from behind and steals the ball from Karl Malone. The Bulls trail by a point. No time-out is called. And here is Jordan on the other end, never doubting himself, isolated on Bryon Russell, allowing the clock to drop below ten seconds, elevating fluently over a flailing Russell, letting go of a picturesque jumper, arm hovering like a beacon as the game-winning shot lands for his sixth NBA championship ring. This is how he walked away, scoring forty-five points, including his team's last eight, frozen in a superlative moment amid the patina of victory. Fade out.

Weeks passed. That image glossed into a portrait in my mind. I thought ahead, about the future, about what would remain of that image a generation from now, if Jordan's legend could persevere. I thought about my children, how their generation had never lived through the careers of Julius Erving and Larry Bird and Magic Johnson, how legacies congeal and grow musty and distant so alarmingly soon.

Part of my work comes as a motivational speaker. I craft my talks around the basic concepts of the human persona: speaking, listening, learning, the elemental skills and traits that shape us. And so I began to build a talk around the legacy of Michael Jordan, monikered after the old advertising slogan: *How to Be Like Mike.*

I spoke to youth groups and corporate leaders. It was a speech that grabbed people, something they wanted to hear. "Can you imagine your organization with Michael Jordans running all over the place?" I'd ask the executives, emphasizing that I wasn't merely talking about the Wednesday night basketball league. I tried to incorporate all that made Jordan one of the transcendent personas of the twentieth century. I've met Jordan a few times, but it was more the testimony of those who knew him that endeared me to the topic. "I'll remember his greatness," Bulls radio announcer Neil Funk told me. "It was like traveling with Babe Ruth. Or Elvis. Or any other great artist."

Jordan is not a flawless man. Because of his extraordinarily public position, his shortcomings were often as widely exposed as his successes. But he is more than merely the sum of his talent, and the lessons of his life are significant enough that they deserve to be compiled here. And they deserve to be emulated. It is my wish that, by the end, you will see there is a way to do this without the benefit of a fadeaway jump shot.

What I give you, then, are eleven chapters that encapsulate a persona as sweeping and immense as any this generation has ever witnessed. Here's hoping that the moment will never fade out.

# CHAPTER ONE

# THE TUNNEL

JORDAN ON FOCUS:

What happens to clutch guys in big moments is that everything slows down. You have time to evaluate the situation, and you can clearly see every move you need to make. You're in the moment, in complete control. It's hard to get there; something has to have you thinking that you can do no wrong. But once you do get there, you can just come out at the start of a game and generate the feeling.

*Concentration is the secret of strength in politics, in war, in trade; in short, in all management of human affairs.*

—Ralph Waldo Emerson

n the morning of Game Five of the 1997 NBA Finals against Utah, during what would be his next-to-last flourish in pro basketball, Michael Jordan was swathed in blankets in a Salt Lake City hotel room, curled into a fetal position, his body limp and wracked with illness. He had a hundred-degree fever. Headaches and nausea had kept him awake all night. He was being pumped with intravenous fluids to replenish his strength.

Word circulated that Jordan was profoundly ill. In the locker room, his teammates surveyed his unusually ashen skin, and television cameras captured Jordan's laconic attempts to practice before the game began.

The Jazz pulled out to an early lead. And yet it was Jordan who kept his team in the game, scoring twenty-one points in the first half, playing nearly the entire second half even as his body began to wither and his energy faded. He hit a three-pointer to give the Bulls the lead, and they won, 90–88. He'd scored fifteen points in the fourth quarter. He'd done it even though he could barely stand. He'd blustered through the malaise, through the breakdown of his body, and he'd maintained his focus on the series, on the game, on his team.

There are a multitude of aspects to the persona that is Michael Jordan: his intelligence, his competitiveness, his perseverance, his leadership. Combined, they are the reason for Jordan's six NBA titles, for his ascendance into the spectrum of the world's most transcendent figures.

But this day in Salt Lake City, Jordan was stripped to his essence. This was Jordan with a singularity of purpose, a focus, that could not be blurred.

The following March, as our team, the Orlando Magic, was arriving for a game in New York, I took a seat on the team bus next to B. J. Armstrong, a veteran guard who played with Jordan in Chicago during their championship run in the early 1990s. It was late, nearly two in the morning, and I had the outline for this book stuffed in my Franklin Planner, which, if you know me, you understand

*Think about MJ's focus. He'd have two or three defenders on him at all times. Think how it must feel to compete against two or three guys every night. He'd face that battle every game.*

—Nate McMillan
HEAD COACH, SEATTLE SONICS

is where I keep everything that is dear to me, except perhaps my children (but only because they couldn't fit). At the time, this book had ten chapters, because motivational speakers like to think in the realm of hard-and-fast numbers.

So I extracted the outline and handed it to B. J. and asked him if he would look it over. He said he would. He took a few minutes as the bus rumbled toward our hotel on 54th Street.

> To focus on what's around you diminishes your ability to focus on what's before you.
>
> —Andy Stanley
> PASTOR AND AUTHOR

Finally, he handed it back to me.

"Looks good," he said. "Looks like you've captured it all."

There was a pause.

"Except you've missed the most important thing."

I nearly choked. "What?" I said. "Tell me, B. J."

"The thing that makes Michael who he is," he said, "is his focus. His ability to concentrate absolutely. To set everything else aside other than what needs to be done right now."

I took the outline into my hotel room and revised and reshuffled for another hour. Which is why you're reading this chapter before the others. Because B. J. Armstrong was right.

> *It is a mistake to look too far ahead. Only one link in the chain of destiny can be handled at a time.*
> —Winston Churchill

"The thing I've noticed about Michael Jordan," says Tom Smithburg, the Bulls' former publicist, "is that he's just completely focused. It's like he's decided to turn on that switch that brings down the curtain and shuts everything out but basketball."

"There was a reason MJ was so focused. He had a routine and nothing could break it. He was never late. He was always extra early. He put his socks on the same way every time, then put on his shorts perfectly. Everything had to be just so," said John Salley, former NBA player.

Smithburg speaks of an invisible "tunnel," of Jordan's ability to walk glassy-eyed through that tunnel from the first day of the season until the last game of the play-offs. He kicked over a garbage can during half-time of a play-off game against Orlando, and it was as if he didn't even realize he'd done it. He's confessed that the games he played were the most serene part of his existence, that he could hear nothing in the tunnel, that he could think prolifically in the midst of that noise.

And it's not that the tunnel affects his demeanor among the public. He's still personable and engaging.

There's just an everlasting sense that the tunnel exists.

"Even when he's smiling and talking to his teammates, or walking through a crowd," Smithburg said, "you know he's in the tunnel, looking toward the end."

"Some athletes have a competitive drive that interferes with their focus," said football coach Bill Walsh. "Very, very few have the complete inventory of qualities: the truly gifted athlete with the truly innate sense of focus. Michael had it—in spades."

The team ophthalmologist for the Bulls and White Sox, David Orth, had a test he used to measure reaction time. A player would peer through a screen into a dark area and Orth would flash sets of numbers on a tic-tac-toe board. They'd appear in increments, from a half-second to one hundredth of a second. The players called out the numbers as they were flashed. Jordan called out more numbers than anyone.

> I coached in the 1988 All-Star game in Chicago. MJ won the slam-dunk contest on that Saturday, but was sick with a bad sore throat. Most guys wouldn't have played in the game on Sunday. MJ went for forty-two against Magic Johnson and the West team.
> —Brendan Suhr
> FORMER NBA ASSISTANT COACH

"What that showed," Orth said, "was spectacular vision. But it was more than that; it showed a tremendous physical ability to concentrate."

> *Success in anything is about focus and concentration. When I coached, I'd say to the players, "Yes, I know you played hard, but that's not good enough. You've got to stay focused on the task at hand the entire game."*
> —Rick Barry
> FORMER NBA STAR

And so Hank Aaron would pull his cap low over his eyes and peer out at troublesome pitchers through a vent in his hat. Broadcaster Ken Venturi insists that you could tell Jack Nicklaus his house was burning down while he stood on the first tee, and he'd shrug and tell you, "I'll take care of it when I get in." Cal Ripken won't read on game days so as not to deplete his daily allocation of focus. Ben Hogan once sank a putt while a train whistle exploded in the distance, and when someone asked him about it, he asked, "What whistle?"

And Michael Jordan became accustomed to the attention in the same ways. He merely factored it in. When team photographer Bill Smith needed to take pictures, Jordan allowed him ten; he'd count them all, and in each he'd give Smith the perfect shot—smiling broadly, eyes wide open and alive. When so many of his games were being broadcast by NBC, Jordan built the pregame interview with the network into his schedule. One day, when NBC decided not to interview him for variety's sake, he approached broadcaster Marv Albert during warm-ups.

"Why didn't we do the interview today?" Jordan said. "You broke up my schedule."

Jordan also knew how to escape the attention. He knew how to hide. He would hole himself up in trainers' rooms and locker rooms before big games, shielding himself from the glare of the moment until it was time to play. Once, before a play-off game, referee Wally Rooney walked into the officials' locker room and found Jordan sitting there. When Rooney asked him what he was doing there, Jordan said, "I had to get away."

In 1998, author Mark Vancil followed Jordan for an entire season while working on a book project. Vancil probed Jordan as thoroughly as he could about the way he handled himself in the midst of those last-second shots. "Don't you feel fear?" Vancil asked "Don't you have negative thoughts?"

To which Jordan replied, "Why would I think about missing a shot I haven't taken yet?"

"Michael had the ability to execute in the moment," Vancil said. "He didn't allow time to wash over itself. He moved through life in step with time, and that was what made him special, more than any physical gift he had. His focus was otherworldly."

> There was a certain amount of fear I took into the games. Not physical fear, but the fear of being humiliated.
> —John Hannah
> FORMER NFL STAR

"The main business," said author Thomas Carlyle, "is not to see what lies dimly at a distance, but to see what lies clearly at hand."

Losing ourselves in the moment. This is focus. My son Stephen once kicked a game-winning goal for his soccer team, and as his teammates mobbed him, he looked confused, even a little stunned. Later, in the car, he admitted that he thought his team trailed 1-0, and that his goal had tied the game. "Talk about a lack of focus," he muttered, without realizing that what he'd done was what few of us have the ability to do, to bury the circumstances, the outside influences, to hone our perspective to a narrow path. Stephen learned a life lesson that day: Everyone pays—either attention or dearly.

"In all the years I coached against MJ, I tried to figure out how we could get to him. I never could find a way. You couldn't get to his mind, his body or his spirit. You just couldn't go at him in any way. He totally perplexed me. He was unattackable. He'd just break guys. I had a deep-seated respect for him," said Pat Riley, head coach of the Miami Heat.

First game of the 1997 NBA Finals at Utah. The Delta Center is tricked up like Barnum and Bailey's Circus: light shows, fireworks, motorcycles, pulsating music, clouds of smoke billowing. The Bulls' players stand in their pregame line, covering their ears, fighting to block out the noise and the colors and the kaleidoscope of distractions. And Utah general manager Scott Layden looked over and saw Jordan, his back to the court, his head bowed, lost in meditation.

"It was chilling," Layden said, "watching him get zoned in like that."

It is the thrust behind the Zen principles that Jordan's coach, Phil Jackson, attempts to impart upon his players. But really, this was not Jackson's influence.

"What did you learn from Phil?" Vancil once asked Jordan.

"I learned that all the Zen stuff Phil had been teaching me," Jordan said, "I'd been doing all my life anyway."

"I never looked at the consequences of missing a big shot," Jordan said. "Why? Because when you think about the consequences, you always think of a negative result. If I'm going to jump into a pool of water, even though I can't swim, I'm thinking about being able to swim enough to survive. I'm not jumping in thinking to myself, 'I think I can swim, but maybe I'll drown.'"

"Focus enabled Michael to step up to another level every day," said NBA coach Lenny Wilkens. "The great ones have this quality. Bird had it. Magic had it. But not at Michael's level."

I have some idea of how exceptional focus in sports can be. Before I discovered my future was in the front office, I played baseball. In all my career, I think I experienced that

> *I remember the time Michael was taping a Chevrolet commercial. The crew was preparing for a long session, a lot of takes. Michael did the whole shoot in one take.*
>
> —Chet Coppock
> BROADCASTER

heightened awareness three times. It was as if the ball appeared to be moving in slow motion, as if I could pick up the path of a curve ball as it left the pitcher's hand, as if I could see the stitches twirl.

Once it happened to me as a senior in high school, in back-to-back games. On a Friday afternoon, I got three hits, two of them home runs. In the next game, the opposing coach (who happened to be my uncle) walked me four times. Once it happened for a whole week in college, at Wake Forest, during a Florida trip my junior year. And once it happened in pro ball, in

> *Michael's ability to nail a commercial spot on the first take was absolutely legendary.*
>
> —Jeff Price
> NBA EXECUTIVE

Miami, when I had four hits in a game at Tampa. I never felt it again in my career. Which explains, once more, why I've spent my career in the front office.

I once asked Philadelphia Phillies' scout Art Parrack, what allowed certain talented players to rise above the others. "Their focus," Parrack said. "Their ability to concentrate on every pitch, every game, every year."

You hear the great athletes speak of it in reverent tones: as if their game is linked to a remote control, slowed down in the midst of chaos, an almost heavenly vision of self-actualization. Bill Russell would talk about this phenomenon in almost spiritual terms.

I have picked up this awful habit late in life of running marathons, a task that requires not only a large amount of self-hatred, but heavy doses of concentration to push through the times when the body begins to break into pieces. In 1998 I was running the Boston Marathon with my wife. We passed the seventeen-mile mark with our feet leaden and our heads dizzy. We passed a woman who held up a sign that shouted in capital letters: FOCUS!

> *If there is any one secret of effectiveness, it is concentration. Effective executives do first things first and they do one thing at a time.*
> —Peter F. Drucker
> AUTHOR

We both lifted our heads and plunged onward. We both finished as the words of Alexander Graham Bell became clear to me: "Concentrate all your thoughts on the task at hand. The sun's rays do not burn until brought to a focus."

"One night I went into the Bulls' locker room in

Denver to talk with MJ. There were about ten writers around him. He said, 'I've got to watch this video.' For the next ten or fifteen minutes, he sat and focused on the Nuggets' last game. We waited. Then he turned to us and focused on our questions," said sportswriter Clay Latimer.

I passed one of our former players, Ben Wallace, in the Magic locker room before a game in 1999 against Golden State. I asked him if he was ready to play.

His eyes bored through me. He was expressionless.

"I'm always ready," he said.

When I met Clarence Weatherspoon, an NBA power forward, I asked him if he had any stories about Jordan. He didn't. Here's why.

"I don't focus on anyone or anything," he said, "except what I'm meant to be doing on the floor."

I thought Michael might appreciate that.

May 17, 1993. Richfield, Ohio. Bulls versus Cavaliers. Almost four years earlier, in this same building, after the Cavs had taken the lead with three seconds to play, Jordan hit a game-winning shot with Craig Ehlo draped on him.

This game is tied. Eighteen seconds left. Jordan: "The fans are booing. They hate me. They're thinking, 'He can't do this to us again.' This one fan under the basket is really

getting ugly, but that's only
helping me to concentrate,
because, you know, God
doesn't like ugly."

Jordan drifts across
the foul lane and sinks a
jump shot. The Bulls
win, 103–101. Again. The
Coliseum is awestruck,

*After the Georgetown–
North Carolina title game
in 1982 where Michael hit
the winning shot. MJ said, "I
could see myself hitting
the shot. I could see it on the
bus, on the way to the
game."*

—John Swofford
FORMER NORTH CAROLINA
ATHLETIC DIRECTOR

silenced. It is not the first time Jordan has cut
through the din of an opposing audience with
unwavering composure. It would not be the last.

Jordan had no tolerance for lapses—from teammates, from coaches, from anyone. He understood
the detriment, even the danger, of divided focus.

Once, during an early season blowout, veteran official Ed Rush's mind began to flit. Jordan could sense
it. During a time-out, he walked over and said, softly,
"Ed, could you let us know when the game is over?
Because we're still playing."

"MJ was focused in the warm-up lines," said NBA
player Billy Owens. "You never saw him smiling in
those lines. He was all business."

Jordan shot 84 percent from the foul line for his
career. Before every one, he spun the ball in his hands.
Then he dribbled until he felt comfortable, somewhere

> *If you chase two rabbits, both will escape.*
> —Ancient Proverb

between three and five times. He spun the ball again. And he shot. "When I'm doing that," he confessed, "I don't see anyone."

Marv Levy, longtime college and NFL coach, tells a wonderful story about focusing on the moment: "I forget where I was, maybe Cal. I was walking up the tunnel, it was a beautiful day, it's a beautiful location, and we were playing Stanford in the Big Game. And I sort of said to myself, 'Man, where else would you rather be than right here, right now?' I got to the sideline before the game and I had the team around, and I could see it in their faces that they felt the same way. And I said it. And from that point I have said it before every kickoff of every game. It's the way I feel."

Karl Wallenda had been walking on high wires for years when he stretched a wire between a pair of buildings in San Juan, Puerto Rico, and attempted to tiptoe across. This was late in his career, and already, Wallenda had seen two relatives die when a seven-person family pyramid toppled. "All Karl thought about, for months, was not falling," said his wife.

It is no surprise, then, that Karl Wallenda fell to his death in San Juan.

So how do we get there, to that place beyond the minutiae of daily life, beyond the noise and distractions of the workplace, beyond the weight of consequence?

The truth is, focus begins with recognition. Of where you are. Of what can be controlled. Of the moments in which we live, and the moments that we can affect. It begins with today.

That's what author Barbara Sher meant when she wrote. "*Now* is the operative word. Everything you put in your way is just another method of putting off the hour when you could actually be doing your dream. You don't need endless time and perfect conditions. Do it now. Do it today. Do it for twenty minutes and watch your heart start beating!"

# Past Performance Is No Guarantee of Future Success

*This is the best day in the history of the world, even though yesterday that seemed an impossibility.*

—Jack Kent Cooke
*sports mogul*

He shocked us more than once. He left basketball for baseball, enduring skepticism and doubt, and he

> *Phil Jackson was always preaching about being in the moment and living for the moment and enjoying each day for what it is.*
> —Steve Kerr
> NBA PLAYER

returned to basketball with a decisive two-word press release—"I'm back." He abandoned the game once again while still near his prime, and he left the placidity of retirement for the challenge of rebuilding a downtrodden Washington Wizards franchise. If there is a thread through Jordan's expansive career, it's that he does what he wants, when he wants, regardless of public perception. He exists in his own moments, carrying ahead into his own select challenges, dedicated toward maximizing life in the present tense.

"Michael taught me to live in the moment. He never talked about the future. If it was the second quarter at Miami, Michael was in the second quarter. He was about right now. Next week's game will take care of itself," said B. J. Armstrong.

* * *

Late in the summer of 1993, Jordan's father, James, pulled his car into a rest stop near Lumberton, North Carolina, to take a respite from the road. Two young men came upon him, murdered him and stole his car.

It had already been a pensive time for Michael Jordan.

Earlier that year, he'd won his third consecutive NBA title, and he'd begun to realize nearly all of his goals in basketball. He'd always been driven by challenges, by the insinuation that he couldn't accomplish something. At first, the media had written that an individual scoring champion couldn't win a team championship. So he won three. Then he wanted to be better than Julius Erving, better than David Thompson, better than Walter Davis, better than Elgin Baylor. He had done it.

But now, no one would deny him anything.

At his father's funeral, Jordan spoke for twenty minutes about relishing the positive aspects of his father's life and avoiding the circumstances that surrounded his death. "We all walked away looking for the positive in this tragedy," said Jordan's friend, Fred Whitfield. "My respect for Michael went way up."

Meanwhile, Jordan took measure of the positives in his own life. The game had become less uplifting, less rewarding. The daily routine had become a chore, and the hubbub surrounding him—in his dealings with the media, in his spectacular array of endorsement contracts—began to wear on him. James Jordan's death only accentuated these points.

"When I did lose the appetite to prove myself again and again," Michael said, "I started tricking myself. I had to create situations to stay on top."

> *Life is always walking up to us and saying, "Come on in; the living's fine." And what do we do? Back off and take its picture.*
>
> —Russell Baker
> AUTHOR

Jordan needed something else. A new situation. He'd hinted before at delving into baseball, his boyhood dream, the sport his father had once believed was his son's best. That summer, he told his personal trainer to begin preparing him for a baseball career.

Baseball, it would seem, was a failure. Jordan never progressed past the Double-A level with the Chicago White Sox. He struggled to hit professional pitching. He barely managed to keep his average above the .200 level in 1994. This was an athlete we were not accustomed to seeing fail, and being at the peak of his fame, in the wake of winning three NBA championships, it only meant the risk he took was that much bigger.

"There was something quite admirable about what he set out to do, a player at the top of his game, a uniquely proud man—arguably the best ever—walking away from one sport and willing to begin at the lower rungs of another very demanding sport, willing to endure the possibility of failure," wrote David Halberstam in his biography of Jordan, *Playing for Keeps.*

BAG IT, MICHAEL, *Sports Illustrated* declared on its cover as Jordan was in the midst of his struggles in baseball. But what *SI* missed, and what all those who peered at Jordan with a jaundiced eye missed, is that even in failure—even when the experiment came to an end and Jordan returned to basketball—he'd succeeded. He'd worked as hard as he could: arriving early for batting practice and staying late. He'd enjoy each moment, his interaction with the young players, the freshness of it, the shifting focus of a career that had otherwise grown stagnant.

"The key is being mentally strong to deal with disappointments, day in and day out, and still having the energy to come back the next day and try to start fresh," Jordan said of his baseball career. "It's very easy to carry things over from game to game, but if you do, it's just going to last a little bit longer."

Winston Churchill believed the key to success was going from failure to failure without losing enthusiasm. And this is the first step toward accentuating our present existence, toward making the most of today. It's why the windshield of your car is ten times the size of the rearview mirror. That's what Ralph Waldo Emerson meant when he wrote, "Write it on your heart that every day is the best day of the year. Finish every day and be done with it. You have done what you could. Some blunders and absurdities no doubt crept in. Forget them as soon as you can; tomorrow is a new day."

There is a line on every mutual fund prospectus that reads: *"Past performance is no guarantee of future success."* It is the story of so many lives, that people either wallow in recent failures or exult in past triumphs so readily that they begin to cloud their present with visions of the past. And they become complacent. They lose sight of the fact that yesterday already happened.

This doesn't mean we should disconnect ourselves entirely from our past. It should be used to help us shape the present that we want. That is, as long as we don't mire ourselves in it.

> *History informs us of past mistakes, from which we can learn without repeating them. It also inspires us and gives us confidence and hope bred of victories already won.*
> —William Hastie
> POLITICIAN AND JUDGE

And so once we've come to terms with our past, there is only a future to confront. It lurks angrily before us, with no promise except uncertainty. It's what Jordan faced in turning to baseball, in risking his reputation, his name, on a romantic risk. He could have hedged. He could have let it go, dismissed it as fantasy, as a pipe dream. But what he had to face couldn't compare to what he might gain. So he dove in.

This is the only way to live, really. Otherwise we make promises to ourselves that we have no real intent of keeping. We become buried in regret, in lost dreams, in the consequence of our actions instead of the joy of them.

"Tomorrow, I don't know what I'm going to do," Jordan said. "I think about today. People don't believe I don't know what's going to happen next week, next month or next year, but I truly live in the moment. I have created the opportunity to have a choice. That is how I'm going to live."

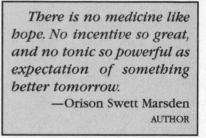

*There is no medicine like hope. No incentive so great, and no tonic so powerful as expectation of something better tomorrow.*
—Orison Swett Marsden
AUTHOR

Of course, it helps to chart our wishes, and make allowances for them so as to always be maximizing our present, guaranteeing our future. It's why some Japanese companies have one-hundred-year plans, and why Walt Disney had what he called a fifty-year master plan.

"Life can be understood by looking backward," said philosopher Søren Kierkegaard, "but it must be lived forward."

Perhaps this may be why since West Point was founded in 1802, only one class has been a staple of the curriculum—map reading. Knowing how to get from here to there is the most important part of any enterprise.

And this is why our goals carry such weight.

# If Only I Had Done This When I Was Young . . .

*Show me a person without goals and I'll show you someone who's dead.*

—George Allen
*former NFL coach*

Susie Maroney had tried it once and failed. She was twenty-two the first time, in June 1996. She'd swam 107 miles in 38½ hours, starting in Cuba, heading across the Straits of Florida toward Key West, banging repeatedly into a cage she'd been swimming inside for protection from sharks. Finally, with her body ravaged by seasickness and dehydration, she collapsed twelve miles from shore.

It was not close enough for Maroney. There was no satisfaction. There was only the thought of bridging those twelve miles, of the goal, of becoming the first woman to swim the Straits of Florida.

Less than a year later, she jumped into the water outside Havana. The seawater bloated her tongue. The fifteen-foot swells toyed with her stomach. Jellyfish stung her repeatedly. The sun wore at her insides like a furnace. The cage battered her skin.

Twenty-four-and-one-half hours later, Maroney emerged on the shore at Key West. As she was talking to reporters, she fainted.

It didn't matter. She'd already made it.

> *Far away, there in the sunshine, are my highest aspirations. I may not reach them, but I can look up and see their beauty, believe in them, and try to follow where they head.*
> —Louisa May Alcott
> AUTHOR

Our goals are what separate us from the wasteland of confused and uncertain voices, from people who hedge and complain and lack faith in themselves. Studies have shown that people who set goals are not merely happier, but more successful. A study of one graduating class at Harvard revealed that only 3 percent of the student body had set clear goals for their future. Twenty years later, the 3 percent had made more money and accomplished more than the other 97 percent combined.

The first setback of Michael Jordan's basketball career has become a treasured anecdote for high-schoolers everywhere. And why shouldn't it? It was the first hurdle Jordan was forced to overcome, when he was cut from the varsity team as a sophomore in high school, and the way he overcame it was simply by concentrating on making the team the next year, by visualizing it, by refusing to fall short of his goal.

"When it happened," he said, "I set another goal . . . a reasonable, manageable goal that I could realistically achieve if I worked hard enough. I approached everything step by step."

> *Success is not a destination; it is a journey. The happiest people I know are those who are working toward specific objectives. The most bored and miserable people I know are those who are drifting along with no worthwhile objectives in mind.*
>
> —Zig Ziglar
> SPEAKER AND AUTHOR

Each challenge was different, another rung in the ladder. Jordan believes, "You have to expect things of yourself before you can do them."

And then there is the story of John Goddard, who, at fifteen years old, heard his grandmother and aunt telling each other, "If only I had done this when I was young . . ." So Goddard sat down and wrote out a list of 127 goals he wanted to accomplish, including seventeen mountains he wanted to climb and ten rivers he wanted to explore. He wanted a career in medicine. He wanted to retrace the travels of Marco Polo and ride a horse in the Rose Bowl Parade, to read the collected works of Shakespeare, to dive in a submarine, to play the flute and violin, to marry and have children.

By the time he was forty-seven, he'd hit 103 of the goals on his list. He became a highly paid lecturer, speaking of his adventures, a walking testament to the value of goal-setting.

Ted Leland, athletic director at Stanford University said, "I know enough about sports psychology to know that athletes who have definite goals tend to succeed better than those with nebulous ambitions." Leland subscribes to the BHAG Theory, taught by author Jerry Porras: "Big, Hairy, Audacious Goals!"

Eight points per quarter. This is all he wanted. For seven consecutive seasons, Jordan's scoring averages were remarkably consistent, all near or above thirty-two points per game. But he never thought of thirty-two points as thirty-two points. He thought of thirty-two points as eight per quarter, and eight per quarter was certainly a manageable number, four field goals in twelve minutes, something he could do rather easily most nights.

In motivational speaking circles, this is called the salami technique, because to contemplate the whole-ness of a goal can often be intimidating, like staring at an entire salami in all of its greasy glory. But cut it into slices, and suddenly each piece becomes its own appetizing entity.

The small battles come first. The mind picks itself up from there. In 1996, at model Margaux Hemingway's funeral in Ketchum, Idaho, her father, Jack, described a story from her childhood as a metaphor for her life, which ended in suicide. Jack said, "Margaux could ski down Bald Mountain faster than anyone. I asked her why she didn't join the junior ski team and she said, 'Dad, when they set the course, I can ski down fast, but when I see the gate, I just can't go through it.'"

Tommy Moe had never won a World Cup skiing event before the 1994 Olympic Games in Lillehammer, Norway. He focused on two minuscule cues: making strong turns on his outside ski, and keeping his hands forward. "I knew if I concentrated on those two things, I would ski fast," he said.

Moe won the gold medal.

My wife, Ruth, who is a speaker for the FranklinCovey Co. and teaches the 7 *Habits of Highly Effective People* class, tells a story about another gold medal winner in the 2000 Summer Olympics— Marion Jones. Her story is also an inspiration, especially for all the female "Mikes" out there. Jones said, "We were raised to believe that anything you wanted in life, you wrote it down. You thought about it, you believed it, and then you went out and got the things you needed to accomplish it. Everything is obtainable." Very few of us twenty-, thirty-, forty-, fifty- or sixty-somethings will ever win Olympic gold medals. But I can win nineteen gold medals in "Dad"; I can win a gold medal in "husband"; I can win a gold medal in "learning" and "health" and "career"—in the things that really matter to me. It's not impossible. But it takes focus, passion, hard work, perseverance, responsibility, leadership, and character. It takes desire. Like Mike, Marion Jones has it. Do you?

While we can *talk* of setting goals, and we can *talk* of achieving them in increments, the truth is that most people still don't make it. The reason is not difficult to ascertain. It's because they get lost in the most difficult aspect of the journey, because they don't have the wherewithal, the self-discipline, to push toward their objective.

Talent matters. Of course it does.

But talent can fizzle without a harness. That's what Bobby Knight meant when he said, "Self-discipline is doing what has to be done; doing it when it has to be done, doing it the best it can be done, and doing it that way every time you do it."

"Michael Jordan is discipline," B. J. Armstrong said. "Not some of the time. Not most of the time. All of the time."

He learned it from his father, and from his coach at North Carolina, Dean

> *We must improve ourselves by victory over ourselves. There must be contests, and we must win.*
> —Edward Gibbon
> HISTORIAN

Smith. Defense, Smith reminded him, was what won games. So Jordan worked on his defense and eventually became the best defensive player in the NBA. Every pickup game, every practice, was an opportunity to improve, to polish the weaker aspects of his game. There was never an acceptance of sufficiency. There was always room for more. "I visualized what I wanted to be," he said. "I knew exactly where I wanted to go."

> *I've never known a man worth his salt who, in the long run, deep down in his heart, didn't appreciate the grind, the discipline. I firmly believe that any man's finest hour, the greatest fulfillment to all he holds dear, is that moment when he has worked his heart out in a good cause, and lies exhausted on the field of battle, victorious.*
> —Vince Lombardi
> HALL OF FAME FOOTBALL COACH

Before Jordan, there was Bill Russell who believed, "You can do anything you set your mind to." You can make an argument that, other than Jordan, no one in the history of basketball was better than Russell, the center for the Celtics. Russell was such a perfectionist he would keep his own personal scorecard for each game. His standards were ridiculously high: twenty-five rebounds, eight assists, eight blocks, 60 percent field-goal percentage. He wanted to run all the plays, to set every pick, to fill the lane properly.

He graded himself from one to one hundred. In

twelve hundred games, he never scored higher than a sixty-five.

The sign on the gate of Tchaikovsky's home warned, "Visiting hours Monday and Tuesday between 3 and 5 P.M. Other times, please do not ring."

He was a composer. Music, not idle conversation, was his gift to the world.

This is discipline.

But what leads us along this path, and what subjects us to such willingness to sacrifice ourselves for our goal? At the essence of a goal fulfilled there is the incandescent ember of something else, the notion that led us here, that holds our heads steady in the midst of the grind.

At the essence of a goal is a dream.

# Of Course I've Got Dreams

*Nothing happens unless first a dream.*
                                                —Carl Sandburg

We can speak all we want in the language of planning and motivation and focus, of maximizing your days and achieving your goals. But none of it means anything if you don't begin with a dream, if there is not a reason to push forward, a reason to concentrate, a reason to discipline yourself.

Susie Maroney wanted to swim. John Goddard wished to experience an adventurous life. And Michael Jordan merely wanted to be recognized as the best basketball player who ever lived.

For some, it starts with that intense vision. For Jordan, it didn't.

"I really didn't know much about professional basketball," he said. "I kept my dreams so much in reach, rather than dreaming about something so far ahead. I kept my dreams closer to me, and more realistic. One step at a time."

> *Don't part with your illusions. When they are gone you may still exist, but you cease to live.*
> —Jonathan Swift
> WRITER

We all dream differently, at varied scales, with diverse focus. The importance is not the range of your dream. The importance is the continued and dogged pursuit of it.

As a student of the self-professed motivational gurus, I spend my time buried in books espousing philosophies and doctrines. And as this book and its eleven-chapter thesis proves, we enjoy formulas. We make our living with lists. I borrow one here, then, from Mike Murdock, who presents fifteen thoughts to help you achieve an uncommon dream:

1. Dreams are born or borrowed.

2. Your dream may require encouragement from others at first.

3. Your dream does not always require the approval of somcone you love.

4. Your dream can start with whatever is in your heart today.

5. You already have what it takes to launch an uncommon dream—DESIRE.

6. Your dream will require a true hunger for attainment

7. Your dream must become your magnificent obsession.

8. Your dream must be energizing enough to cause you to make a change in your daily routine.

9. An uncommon dream will require immediate attention.

10. Your dream deserves your total focus.

11. Your dream may require a geographical change.

12. Your dream will always require the assistance of others.

13. Your dream may require extraordinary negotia-
    tions with others.

14. You must always build your daily agenda
    around your dream.

15. You must nurture and protect those relation-
    ships connected to your dream.

Now read this list again. Pause after each one, and think
of Michael Jordan, of what we've discussed, of what we
know about this man, of the encouragement he received,
of the desire he emanated, of the "magnificent obsession,"
of the "total focus." It all
seems to fit, doesn't it?

> *I don't design clothes. I
> design dreams.*
> —Ralph Lauren

It's a dream, after all,
that blesses us with the
focus to block out everything else. It's the realization
of a dream that affords us true bliss, as basketball did
for Michael Jordan.

And what keeps those dreams in the box? What
produces such self-consciousness?

Often, it's merely a realization. It's the understanding that we can't control the path of our dreams, that
sometimes they become derailed by events or actions
that we cannot affect. This devastates us. This forces
us back into the box. And this destroys the whole

process. And in the end, it
might destroy us.

One of my favorite
writers, the late Erma

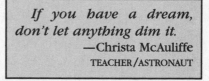

> *If you have a dream,*
> *don't let anything dim it.*
> —Christa McAuliffe
> TEACHER/ASTRONAUT

Bombeck, observed: "There are people who put their
dreams in a little box and say, 'Yes, I've got dreams, of
course I've got dreams.' Then they put the box away
and bring it out once in a while to look at it, and yep,
they're still there. These are great dreams, but they
never even get out of the box. It takes an uncommon
amount of guts to put your dreams on the line, to hold
them up and say, 'How good am I or how bad am I?'"

## It's out of Your Hands

*I play the game over in my mind and get out of*
*it what I can. I'll think about it for a while, then*
*let it go. I'm strong enough mentally to put it*
*away.*

—Michael Jordan

There are times when it's not our fault, times when
we've done everything to prepare for the moment, to
enjoy the flush of success, and we fall short. Every

shot Jordan took had such immense preparation behind it. And yet his career field-goal percentage was barely above fifty percent. Which means he failed half the time, sometimes even in weighty moments, late in the game or deep in the postseason.

But there was always a next time. And he had the fortitude to shake off the daunting notion of failure, to take the same shot again, to recognize that our destiny is not always under our own power.

In sports, in business, in life, we have a tendency to blame ourselves when something goes wrong. We assume we control everything about our professional lives, and we become mired in self-doubt. And while we flounder, our dreams continue to tiptoe above our grasp.

Remember what you can't control: death, undeserved criticism, a job transfer, illness. And remember what you can control: your time, your effort, your thoughts, your tongue, your attitude, your choice of friends, your commitments, your response to failure.

You can always count on baseball players for pithy philosophies, if nothing else. Here, then, in that great Yogi Berra tradition, is former outfielder Mickey Rivers:

"Don't worry about things you have no control over, because you have no control over them," he says.

"Don't worry about the things that you have control over, because you have control over them."

\* \* \*

One of the measures of Jordan's impact is that everyone who met him seems to carry away a story. For Mary Lou Retton, the Olympic gymnast, it came when she asked about the death of his father, about how he dealt with the pain and the loss.

Jordan shrugged. Said he did the best he could with it. Tried to take something positive away. "I had him for thirty-one years," he said. "Some people don't even have a father for two or three."

There was nothing he could do. He couldn't bring his father back. He couldn't prevent the crime, couldn't lash out anymore at the men who'd committed the crime. It was characteristic of Jordan's acceptance of the random order of events, and his recognition of that which he couldn't alter.

Of course, the common reaction to unalterable courses of events—to delays, to market fluctuations, to trends, to the action of our competitors—is panic or rage or despair. We overreact, unspooling our

> *Immense power is acquired by assuring yourself, in your secret reveries, that you were born to control affairs.*
>
> —Andrew Carnegie
> INDUSTRIALIST

emotions, unraveling our concentration. We lose our train of thought. We lose sight of our direction.

"My grandparents always used to say, 'Think before you act, and be in control at all times,'" Jordan said. "I always remembered that. You forget about the outcome. You know you are doing the right things, so you relax and perform. After that, you can't control anything anyway. It's out of your hands, so don't worry about it."

All it can do is shatter your focus. All it can do is cloud your dreams.

# CHAPTER TWO

# THE JOY

JORDAN ON PASSION:

A lot of us in the NBA, we take it for granted that this is the only place we can play basketball, because we've made it to here. We forget about what it felt like when we were playing in high school, when it was so exciting just to put on that uniform and go onto the court for the game. Those days felt just as good as a lot of days in the NBA feel. Maybe better, because we didn't take it for granted.

*My advice to kids is to let them just enjoy the game. Develop a love for the game.*

—Michael Jordan

he feeling first overcame him in the back-yard, on the court his father built in Wilmington, North Carolina, in the midst of brutal one-on-one games against his older brother, Larry. It was there that Michael Jordan fell in love with basketball. He delighted in his improvement, in his first victories against a sibling who once had over-powered him. He spent hours on that court, until he was good enough to make his high school team, until he blossomed into a star.

Those early glimpses of his potential were a revelation for Jordan. "He knew that he was going to get better," says Buzz Peterson, who roomed with Jordan at a high school basketball camp and later played with him at North Carolina. "For the first time he had a sense of what the future might bring for him—and he was in love with it."

Jordan kept those diligent habits as his notoriety grew, as the temptations to succumb to distraction swelled around him. Every practice was a source of enthusiasm; games were punctuated by a grin, by a helpless shrug of the shoulders as another three-point shot faded into the net. Didn't matter if it was a tepid evening in January against the Clippers or the heightened tension of a finals game against Utah, Jordan was there every night, pushing, prodding, elevating the moment. He was a relentless talker, always dancing along the edges of cockiness, yet able to sharpen that edge by backing up his attitude.

A reporter once asked Luc Longley, Jordan's teammate in Chicago, what it was that amplified Jordan's game, what made him such a rarity. Longley was a rangy center for the Bulls, an Australian of moderate talent who was often the victim of Jordan's

> *When I was in college at Xavier, I saw an MJ quote in* Jet *magazine: "I play for the love of the game, not for the love of money." I went and got a tattoo on my chest because of that. It says, "For the Love."*
> —Michael Hawkins
> NBA PLAYER

consistent urgings. And to the reporter, Longley replied, in his rich Australian accent, "Michael Jordan is always up."

For eighty years, a cellist named Pablo Casals began every morning with the same exacting routine. He'd walk to his piano, play two preludes and fugues of Bach, and let the music flood over him, a sort of benediction, a daily rediscovery, an ode to the brilliant hues of life.

I imagine that, with the same feeling coursing through him each morning, Jordan picked up a basketball, spun it in his fingers, set his feet, dribbled two or three times and took his first shot.

Meanwhile, amid joyous lives like Jordan's, there are large portions of our society who toil in futility, long ago accepting of their own mediocrity. They accede to other's wishes, barely twitching a finger to change things. They bury themselves in the boredom and monotony of the everyday with nothing but an ineffable vision of what might come next.

> *You've achieved success in your field when you don't know whether what you're doing is work or play.*
>
> —Warren Beatty
> ACTOR

Perhaps we know people like this. Perhaps we *are* people like this: devoid of the passion and energy that carries us from one moment to the next, unable to combat the intangible force that sets roadblocks in our minds. And then one lonesome afternoon in a corner office, it floods us: the pain, the anguish, the irreversible regret for what we should have done and never did, because we followed the path to comfort instead of the path to our yearnings.

And we wind up lost, buried in our own remorse.

But here's the thing: It's never too late for recovery.

# The Glow of Enthusiasm

There is an energy that spills from the eyes of a joyous person, that emanates from their cheerful and exaggerated motion. But it's more than just a surface energy that they're revealing. What matters is what's below, because the starriness of a person like this reveals so much about their potential for success. They are people doing what they want to do, living how they want to live, people who dictate their own actions, people who are immersed in their greatest pleasures: hitting a baseball, playing a trumpet, writing, drawing, painting, shooting a basketball.

> *This was when I was with the Philadelphia 76ers. I was sitting on the bench and MJ came dribbling past us at full speed. Then he shifted into another gear and went to the hoop. I'll never forget that fire in his eyes, that look of determination. It scared me to see that look. I've never seen it before. I've never seen it since.*
>
> —Roy Hinson
> FORMER NBA PLAYER

Historian David McCullough observed, "I would pay to do what I do. People say, 'Take a vaction,' How could I have a better time than what I am doing?"

Author Laurence Sterne writes in *A Sentimental Journey*: "What a large volume of adventures may be grasped within this little span of life by him who interests his heart in everything."

"You have to find something that you love enough to be able to take risks, jump over the hurdles and break through the brick walls that are always going to be placed in front of you," said movie director George Lucas. "If you don't have that kind of feeling for what it is you're doing, you'll stop at the first giant hurdle."

Author Roger Kahn once called Willie Mays the most joyous ballplayer of his era, especially at the prime of his career, in 1954, his first year back from duty in the army, when the Giants won the pennant. Mays couldn't wait to get to the ballpark. He had the same anxious feeling each day. "You got to love the game," he said. "Else how you gonna play good?"

And some years later, Willie Mays observed Michael Jordan, his serpentine creative moves in traffic, his relentless bursts of vigor, his eponymous grin. "I look at Michael and I see a player who loves basket- ball," Mays said. "He loves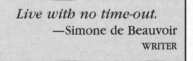

*Live with no time-out.*
—Simone de Beauvoir
WRITER

playing it the way I loved playing baseball. In- telligence, sure, but love is a big reason Michael can play basketball the way he does."

Jordan is the only player I know of who had a "Love of the Game" clause inserted into his contract; it

> *I watched hours and hours of MJ on tape. He never relented for a second. He never took a play off. He was on all the time. Always wired up.*
>
> —Brendan Malone
> NBA ASSISTANT COACH

meant he could play in any basketball game at any time, whenever he wanted, without getting approval from the team.

Again I take you back to Jordan in college at North Carolina, to his days under Dean Smith, who used to insist that both he and his assistant coaches maintain a vigorous demeanor throughout practice, and that his players do the same. This way, he figured, even if someone wasn't charged that day, even if a player felt like someone had removed his batteries, they'd be so coerced into enthusiasm that they'd end up feeling it regardless.

Amid those practices, Jordan would dive for loose balls, would skin knees, would fight for every rebound. During one-on-one drills he'd spill with an almost boyish brashness, teasing his teammates as he'd drive by them, time after time, for easy dunks. Afterward, he'd write their names on a blackboard, with Roman numerals next to each name. The numerals signified how many times Jordan had dunked on them that afternoon.

He meant nothing personal by it. It was just a mischievous incarnation of Jordan's ardor for the game.

Former teammate Ed Nealy said, "They should've charged admission for every Bulls practice, because you'd have seen more from Michael there than in the games. It didn't matter if we'd played five games in eight days. MJ would practice like it was his last day in uniform."

From the beginning of his NBA career, Jordan was the first to show up at practice and the last to leave. If there was a weakness in his game when he came to the NBA, it was that his jump shot was only slightly above average. So he'd work on his jump shot for hours with coach Kevin Loughery. They'd bet on games of HORSE, until Jordan could win back his money after Loughery tired out.

Wrote David Halberstam: "He was going to be a great player, Loughery thought, not just because of the talent and the uncommon physical aspects but because he loved the game. That love could not be coached or faked, and it was something he always had. He was joyous about practices, joyous about games, as if he could not wait for either."

> *From the glow of enthusiasm, I let the melody escape. I pursue it. Breathless, I catch up with it. It flies again. It disappears; it plunges into a chaos of diverse emotions. I catch it again. I seize it. I embrace it with delight.... I multiply it by modulations and at last I triumph in the first theme. There is the whole symphony.*
> —Ludwig van Beethoven

"In 1992 at the Barcelona Olympics, we played cards until six in the morning," said Magic Johnson. "MJ got one hour of sleep, then played eighteen holes of golf. That night he scored twenty-eight points. After the game, we played cards all night. Then golf at eight in the morning. On the third night, MJ said, 'We're staying up all night playing cards.' I said, 'MJ, I can't do it. I can't do what you do. I've got to get some sleep.'"

There was so much joy that Jordan could manage to play extensive rounds of golf the day before a crucial playoff game and emerge from the locker room with the same energy level. He could subsist on two or three hours of sleep a night. In the 1992 Olympics in Barcelona, as Magic Johnson said, Jordan played thirty-six holes each day, a game at night and then sometimes played cards until six in the morning. Finally, when the U.S. was due to face its toughest opponent, Russia, U.S. Coach Chuck Daly went to Jordan and said, "MJ, how about you play eighteen holes today?"

> It is the greatest shot of adrenaline to be doing what you've wanted to do so badly. You almost feel like you could fly without the plane.
>
> —Charles Lindbergh
> AVIATOR

Jordan agreed. That night he locked down one of Russia's best players, Sarunas Marciulionis. The U.S. won easily. Afterward, Jordan said to Daly, "I could

have played another
eighteen holes today."

Sports columnist Mark
Whicker said, "Michael's
energy level was just different. He couldn't relax.

> *When you have the chal-
> lenge, you feel the hunger
> for the game, the love for the
> game, the attitude of com-
> ing in and working harder
> in practice.*
> —Michael Jordan

Even his relaxation was strenuous."

"He has a great sense of humor," said former Bulls
trainer Mark Pfeil. "And he has that big grin all the time."

During his rookie season, when it's customary for
most players to wear down physically, Jordan would
often scoff at the trainers' concern for his fatigue
level. Can you play this many minutes, the trainers
would ask. Do you need a break?

Jordan would grin. "Watch me," he'd say.

"Michael Jordan's energy supply is what separates
him from other people," says Bulls assistant coach Bill
Cartwright. "Nobody in the NBA has as much energy.
I believe that enthusiasm finds the opportunities and
energy makes the most of them."

"In 1984, Michael played in the Olympics and then
reported to the Bulls camp as a rookie," said Jordan's
former teammate, Sidney Green. "All the vets thought
he'd be tired and wouldn't have any legs. He started
camp by outrunning and outjumping all of us. Then,
the second week, he ran even faster and jumped

higher. By mid-season, he'd gone to an even higher level. He wanted to prove to everyone how special he was—and he was. He was the truth, the whole truth, and nothing but the truth."

I am known to those around me as a rather enthusiastic person—a notion that most would probably consider a vast understatement. Throughout the course of my career in the front office in both minor-league baseball and the NBA, my energy has led me to some rather odd precipices. Wrestling bears, for instance. Or overseeing the most disappointing trained pig act in the history of Philadelphia sports. Or donning a sweaty mascot's suit. All for the sake of entertainment.

Some might call me crazy. I call it a surplus of joy. And I just happen to believe you should have enough of a surplus to fill a Wal-Mart.

> *The aim of life is to live, and to live means to be awake, joyously, drunkenly, serenely, divinely awake.*
> —Henry Miller
> WRITER

It's something I learned from my mentor, a one-legged baseball executive named Bill Veeck, who earned a measure of fame for having the courage and ingenuity to let a midget bat during a major-league baseball game. Veeck was the sort of man who slept two hours a night, whose head exploded with ideas. He was flush with energy. He relished interaction, and he savored the small pleasures of his life in baseball. And of his life outside of baseball. When Bill died in 1986, sports columnist Thomas Boswell wrote: "Cause of death—life."

These are the people I admire, the ones who leave nothing ambiguous. Musicians like Ella Fitzgerald and Louis Armstrong exuded a

> *Catfish Hunter stuffed twenty pounds of life into a five-pound sack. His life was a charm bracelet of good times.*
>
> —Steve Rushin
> SPORTSWRITER

spontaneous optimism on stage; Ted Williams was nicknamed "The Kid" for the way he bounced from the dugout each afternoon. Thomas Edison sacrificed fortunes for the sake of continuous time to invent; Charles Schulz drew his *Peanuts* comic strip until the months before his death because it was all he could imagine. Tina Turner still struts on stage, even now that she's well past fifty—"When you're around Tina," said talk-show host Oprah Winfrey, "you say, 'I want some of that energy that's coming off her.'" John Madden has said he could broadcast pro football games for an eternity; one of my favorite public speakers is former Dodgers manager Tommy Lasorda, who could probably weave stories for an eternity; and Joe Paterno seems destined to coach college football at Penn State for an eternity. "I've never been bored,"

> *In 1981, I played with MJ at the McDonald's High School All-America game in Wichita. First practice, I was stunned. MJ got off the bus and without warming up, he was running and dunking all over the place.*
> —Chris Mullin
> NBA PLAYER

Paterno said. "Maybe that's part of the reason I stay in it." Baltimore Ravens coach Brian Billick said it best: "Passion is the lubricant of success."

Not long ago, my wife Ruth and I were in Manhattan, preparing to perform another of our insane, enthusiastic stunts: running the New York City Marathon. The day before the race, we stopped into a Barnes and Noble bookstore where we had a chance to meet syndicated columnist George Will. We told him we were there to run the marathon.

He looked at us solemnly, his face blank and curious. He said, "Why?"

I've thought a great deal about that question. Why? I don't know why. It's uncontrollable. It's an urge, a passion, something that blossoms from deep within and won't let me stop.

It may be the most consequential advice we can pass along to our children: To find something they love, to chase after it and to savor its every twist. My son Bobby was scrawling major-league starting line-ups on notepads when he was six; now he works as a coach in the Cincinnati Reds farm system. As a boy,

A. J. Foyt was racing around the outside of his house in a child-size racing car. And Wayne Gretzky, at three years old, was watching hockey games while flopping around in stockinged feet on a linoleum floor. He would cry when the game ended, unable to comprehend the deprivation of this one exalted joy. On the day that forty-six-year-old Moses Malone was voted into the Basketball Hall of Fame, he was on his way to a Houston recreation center for a 1 P.M. pick-up game.

A magazine called *Nation's Business* once surveyed its readers, attempting to extract the top ten businesspeople America had poured forth in its first two hundred years. The list included the names you'd expect: Edison, Henry Ford, Alexander Graham Bell. But what's interesting is that while each of the ten choices was involved in highly competitive businesses—often cited as a cause of health problems—they lived ripely to an average age of eighty-seven.

> *MJ, I guess, had decided he'd catch up on sleep some other time in his life.*
> —Matt Geiger
> NBA PLAYER

Another survey polled 241 executives on the traits that most helped workers to become a success. More than 80 percent listed "enthusiasm." Second, at 63 percent, was a "can-do attitude."

And enthusiasm does spread. If we project it, say, at

> *MJ brought out the fire in everyone around him. He never missed a practice, no matter how many minutes he played the night before, no matter how many points he scored. That attitude, that pattern, spread to the rest of us.*
>
> —Scott Burrell
> NBA PLAYER

a board meeting or in a presentation, it will carry through the room. Remember that groups aren't naturally enthusiastic about doing anything. I've seen this in my flock of nineteen children (sixteen of whom were teenagers at the same time), whose primary pastime seems to be sitting on the couch complaining about the lack of things to do in life, because nothing in life is cool enough to do. It's the same with a company. It's the same with a team. We turn to leaders because they press us into action, because they make us feel that what we're doing is healthy and intriguing and challenging. As long as that feeling is authentic, as long as it is not hidden from view, we can inspire entire groups.

How many teams did Jordan improve just by being there? How many others' games did he inspire? In his book, Halberstam makes mention of Steve Hale, another of Jordan's teammates at Carolina, a player of marginal ability who subsisted mostly on hustle. Jordan did the same. Every loose ball Jordan rushed after, every extra effort he made during practice, only further endeared him to the teammates who weren't blessed with his natural ability. And it only made them want what Jordan wanted that much more fervently.

Bill Russell believed, "Hustle is a talent."

Former major-league baseball player Gene Woodling said, "You don't tell me to hustle. That's an insult. I never wanted to hear a ballplayer saying, 'Nice hustling.' You're supposd to do that, and I did."

> *I always told the musicians in my band to play with what they know, and then to play above that. Because anything can happen, and that's where great art and music happens.*
> —Miles Davis
> JAZZ MUSICIAN

## "I Won't Be a Bitter Old Man"

*You've got to get obsessed and stay obsessed.*
—John Irving
*writer*

But let's say something's missing. Let's say you don't share this feeling. Let's say you're swept up in the modern malaise of our culture, the dour and cynical cult of people who, as sociologist Tony Campolo suggested, don't dance, don't sing and are "becoming emotionally dead."

What then?

> *People don't choose careers. They're engulfed by them.*
> —John Dos Passos
> WRITER

The only intervention is to discover a passion in life. I cannot tell you where to find it. I can only tell you that it is absolutely crucial that you find it, wherever you have to go, whatever sacrifices you have to make, whatever risks you may incur. It's the only way. Because I can guarantee that what you're lacking is not intelligence, not education, not training. What you're lacking is that fire, that certainty of action that branches forth from those early musings of energy and enthusiasm. What you're crippled by is a lack of purpose.

Hockey's Gordie Howe stated, "If you're not in love with what you're doing, just move over and make room for somebody who is."

And why aren't we engulfed by our careers? Why do we lack passion? Here, courtesy of author Greg Morris, are four possible maladies:

**Routine**—We allow something precious to become familiar. This was Jordan in the aftermath of his father's death, his senses dulled by basketball, his focus nosing elsewhere, eventually choosing baseball for a shake-up.

**Acceptance and approval**—Passion both draws and repels people. Some are attracted to clarity of focus, and others are threatened by it. This means that

> *If you are going to try to persuade others to go with you, it certainly doesn't hurt that you've got very strong convictions about where you are going. Like Columbus did, for instance, to discover the New World. And if you've got passion and conviction, you're more likely to be inspiring. If you're inspired yourself and you're passionate about something, you're more likely to get others to come with you.*
>
> —Ted Turner
> MEDIA EXECUTIVE

there are times when we feel as if we have to protect ourselves from others' skepticism, when our passion may seem misplaced. And so we mask it for the sake of consent.

**Apathy increases with age**—As we grow older, it is harder to contain our skepticism.

**We have no purpose beyond ourselves**—We lose sight of possibility, of the impact we may have on others. And without those notions, we're condemned to skepticism.

"You're only bitter if you reach the end of your life and you're filled with frustration because you feel you missed out on something," Jordan said. "You're bitter because you regret not accomplishing things you could have accomplished. I won't be a bitter old man."

"Michael has passion," says his ex-teammate, B. J. Armstrong, "and you have to have that same passion, that same will, to beat him. He prepares himself in a way that no one will understand, because I don't think too many people are willing to pay that price."

> *Enjoy every minute of life. Never second-guess life.*
> —Michael Jordan

In 1984, before he joined the Bulls, before he began his glorious professional career, Jordan had one last amateur experience: the 1984 Olympics in Los Angeles. His coach was Bob Knight, and one of the first things Knight did when pulling his team together was to recognize Jordan's leadership qualities, his overriding passion. Before the competition began, he pulled Jordan aside and told him he might make an example of him as a way to motivate some of the less driven players on the team.

The morning of the gold-medal game, Knight had prepared an elaborate pep talk, full of hyperbole and euphemisms. But when he walked into his office that day, someone had dropped a yellow piece of paper on his chair.

"Coach," it said. "Don't worry. We've put up with too much garbage to lose now."

It was signed, "The Team."

The Team, Knight understood, was Jordan. And so Knight never gave his speech. He never had to.

The USA led Spain by twenty-seven points at half-time, and Knight leaned over to Jordan and shouted at him, as a ploy to avoid a second-half slump, "When are you going to start setting some screens?"

Jordan smiled. "Coach," he said, "didn't I read some place where you said I was the quickest player you ever coached?"

"Yeah," Knight said. "What's that got to do with it?"

"Coach, I set those screens faster than you could see them."

> Michael Jordan is one of the greatest competitors I've ever seen in any sport. And he looks like he's always enjoying it.
>
> —John Wooden
> BASKETBALL COACH

Lesser players with lesser resolves and flagging spirits have slogged amid Knight's prickly nature, disturbed by his constant ribbing. Not Jordan. In the grizzled eye of the beast, he made heady pro-nunciations and cracked bold one-liners, engulfed and shielded by his passion for the game.

# CHAPTER THREE

# THE HARD WAY

JORDAN ON WORK:

You can't turn it on and off like a faucet. I couldn't dog it during practice and then, when I needed that extra push late in the game, expect it to be there. But that's how a lot of people approach things. And that's why a lot of people fail. They sound like they're committed to being the best they can be. But when it comes right down to it, they're looking for reasons instead of answers.

*Don't wish it were easier. Wish you were better.*

—Jim Rohn
*author and speaker*

s the dutiful, sometimes distracted and rather harried father of nineteen—yes, you are reading that right—biological and adopted children, it is an element of my duty to douse the fires that sprout forth in youth. So a few months ago I made a speaking appearance in Gainesville, Florida, then went off to fulfill my commitment as a father by springing for dinner for my twin South Korean sons, Thomas and Stephen, who were mired in summer school at the University of Florida.

We met at a Mexican restaurant. We sat, and as the waitress slid bowls of nacho chips and salsa in front of us, I asked how school was going, and the trouble began.

"Dad," Stephen said, "Thomas isn't doing so well."

I turned to Thomas. He said nothing. So I turned back to Stephen. "Since you seem to be your brother's spokesman this evening," I said, "perhaps you can tell me why he's not doing so well."

"Thomas is burned out," Stephen said.

I pivoted back to Thomas, who wore a despondent frown. He nodded. "Dad," he said, "I'm burned out on school."

"So?" I said.

"So I think I need a summer off."

*Burned out?* I thought. Thomas was taking a few paltry summer session credits, and he was burned out. I straightened. My voice tightened, wrapped in the paternally stern tone of a father who had heard this a thousand times before.

"Tom," I said. "Get over it."

Before he could speak again, I was in the midst of a rather dutiful lecture about responsibility, about dedication, about the constancy of work. "I haven't had a summer off in forty-five years," I said. "And neither will you. So get used to it."

I am happy to report that Thomas got an A in summer school. And neither he nor Stephen will ever dare to use the phrase "burned out" in my presence again.

# Genius, Upgrading Genius

Michael Jordan's sophomore year at North Carolina ended with the Tar Heels losing to Georgia in the

NCAA Tournament's Elite Eight. There were four weeks left in the semester, and Dean Smith went out of town to recruit, leaving Roy Williams in charge. "The big push has to be on school," Smith told Williams. "No basketball. And besides, they're tired. They need a break."

So Williams met with Jordan and told him to shut down for a while. Jordan agreed. "I've been playing ball for three years without a break," he said. "I need to get fresh."

At lunch that day, Williams went for a run. Afterward, in the locker room, he saw Jordan, walking past with a ball in his hands.

"I thought you were resting," Williams said.

"Coach," Jordan said, "I can't do it. I've got to work on my game."

"In 1985, after Jordan was named NBA rookie of the year, he came back to Chapel Hill and said to Roy Williams, 'I've got to talk to you,'" said Jordan biographer David Halberstam. "Roy said, 'Sure, Mike.' Michael said, 'No, coach. In private.' They went out to the bleachers and Michael said, 'Coach, what do I have to do to get better?' No player worked like Michael."

> *Michael had that rare capacity to be a genius who wanted to upgrade his genius.*
> —John Bach

The first Bulls practice after Jordan made his

> *The coaching got better in the Eastern Conference, because we put in so much time thinking, studying and preparing for MJ.*
> —Jeff Van Gundy
> HEAD COACH, NEW YORK KNICKS

comeback to basketball in 1995 ended with Michael walking to the baseline, on his own, and running windsprints. Without a word, all eleven of his teammates joined him.

Former Bulls assistant coach John Bach had a term for it, for Jordan's perpetual willingness to labor at the game. "Vaulting ambition," he called it, and what he meant was that every year Jordan would spend the off-season improving portions of his game that he felt were lacking, so that he could more readily play through fatigue, through pain, through illness. He improved his ball-handling. He became a defensive stopper and a perennial member of the NBA All Defensive First Team. He improved his shooting, staying late at practice, challenging the long-range shooters until he was good enough to shoot in the NBA All-Star Game's three-point contest. When his body wore down against thicker opponents, he began lifting weights so he could handle himself in the low post. Toward the end of his career, during the summer he made the movie *Space Jam*, Jordan had a court put up on the set, which is where he developed a wicked fallaway jumper that became his latter-day trademark. When he found out Scottie Pippen could dunk with his left hand, he learned to do it himself. "Michael was always trying to figure out how to turn his weaknesses into strengths," said Phil Jackson.

Michael once observed, "I have always approached practice as a kind of proving ground, especially with rookies. They might have seen me on television, read about me . . . and might think they know what I'm all about. . . . I want them to know it isn't gossip or rumors. I want them to know it all comes from hard work. Every time I stepped on the court, even though I was on top of the world, I felt like I had something to prove."

> *Success isn't something you have to put forth the effort for constantly; then maybe it'll come when you least expect it. Most people don't understand that.*
> —Michael Jordan

"We fight human nature in this business," said NBA assistant coach Jim Boylen. "It's the 'Get-By' Theory: most guys will work just as hard as they must in order to achieve success. Michael fought human nature. Despite his success, he never got comfortable or satisfied. He always needed more."

"Michael had a rare quality—a sense of how good he would become," said David Halberstam. "And he knew he'd have to pay the price to do the things he wanted to do on the court."

Somebody asked Jordan, after he won his fifth championship in 1997, why he'd bother to keep playing. "Because," he said, "I still think I can get better."

> *The average person puts only 25 percent of his energy and ability into his work. The world takes off its hat to those who put in more than 50 percent of their capacity, and stands on its head for those few and far between souls who devote 100 percent.*
>
> —Andrew Carnegie
> INDUSTRIALIST

The National Commission on Productivity once found that only two of every ten employees work to their full potential, and that half of the workforce expends only the minimum amount of energy needed to get by. Which means there are great and expansive numbers of our workforce (perhaps even some at the National Commission on Productivity) who waste their days attempting to shake an extra Three Musketeers bar from the vending machine, or who hide behind the walls of their cubicle playing Tetris.

Which makes those of us who actually do throw ourselves into work that much rarer, that much more valuable, that much more inclined toward success. One author's study of self-made millionaires revealed, rather unsurprisingly, that none of them were among those who worked a pedestrian forty hours a week or less, fighting away the cobwebs of boredom while clocking in and out.

It was not uncommon for Jordan to become embroiled in fights during practice. He didn't tolerate mediocrity, even on a lazy midseason afternoon with nothing at stake. He had this need to establish himself, to elevate himself and to prove himself with every drill, as if, at all times, his reputation was perched over a pot of boiling water, on the verge of withering. At North Carolina, he'd stay after practice and challenge his teammates to one-on-one contests. Shooting, dunking, dribbling. He'd stay until he won something.

> *Few people, during their lifetime, come anywhere near exhausting the resources dwelling within them. There are deep wheels of strength that are never used.*
>
> —Richard Byrd
> REAR ADMIRAL

The day after North Carolina lost to Indiana in the NCAA Tournament, ending Jordan's junior year—the year after Williams first advised him to take a break—he was once again in the gym, practicing. Later that spring, his Carolina teammate, Steve Hale, saw Jordan in the gym, playing in a pick-up game with nine fraternity guys. "Why bother?" Hale asked.

"Working on my game," Jordan replied.

Always. During the season, during the off-season;

even now, in retirement, he continues to push himself. In shootarounds, he would arrive five minutes earlier than everyone else and stay five minutes later. Once, in San Antonio, says former NBA coach Bob Hill, Jordan rode a bike to a health club to lift weights, then rode the bike back to the Alamo Dome in time for practice. The day after the now-immortalized "Sick Game" in Utah, Jordan spent ninety minutes in the gym.

"I would use one word to describe Michael," said Charles Barkley. "*Obsessive*. He was obsessed with being the greatest player possible. Everything he did was designed to be done better than anyone else."

> *One of the rules I have for myself when I work out is that I'm always going to be the last player off the field. If I've been taking grounders for two minutes or twenty minutes, and another player comes out to join me, I'll stay on the field and continue working until he's done.*
>
> —Derek Jeter
> NEW YORK YANKEES SHORTSTOP

"In 1984, when we were on the Olympic team together," said University of Iowa basketball coach Steve Alford, "MJ would always play after practice with Chris Mullin or me. He knew we could shoot, and shooting was the weak point of his game. By the end of the summer he was winning most of the games of HORSE we played. He amazed me. He worked so hard, even though he didn't have to."

On the day of a game against Barkley and the Phoenix Suns in 1993, broadcaster Nick Pinto got to Chicago Stadium early in the afternoon to deliver some tapes. There, on the court, hours before tip-off, was Michael Jordan.

"He's been here all day," a security guard said. "Shooting free throws."

There is a story about a trip to Boston during Jordan's rookie season that coach Stan Albeck likes to tell. Albeck had the bus arrive at Boston Garden early one day. He had a reason for doing it. He was doing it for Michael. He led the team inside. The Garden was empty and silent. Then, from nowhere, they heard footfalls, and when they looked up, they saw Larry Bird running the concourse. Then running the steps. Bird worked up a sweat, then began shooting. Jordan's eyes glazed over. "You could see then," said Albeck, "that he knew that was what it took."

That same year, when Jordan hurt his foot, he came back to Chapel Hill to do his rehab work. Every morning, former Carolina assistant Randy Weil would look out his office window and see Jordan, working on the same moves again and again. "In the game it looks like he's just reacting," Weil said, "but I know differently."

He studied all of the game's anomalies. When the Bulls moved from Chicago Stadium to the United

Center, players began to get the sense that the rims on the baskets were stiff, and this made the shooting tougher. Early one afternoon, sportswriter Kent McDill showed up for a game and found Jordan out there, studying the rims. He'd shoot, miss, slam dunk, and hang on the rim, trying to loosen it up, to solve the puzzle, to develop the smallest advantage.

> *The tougher you are on yourself, the easier life will be on you.*
> —Zig Ziglar

Once, at a basketball camp, an attendee asked him, "How many hours did you practice as a kid?"

"I never worried about time," Jordan replied. "I never watched the clock. I practiced until I got tired or until my mama called me for dinner."

"The 1984 Olympic team was playing an exhibition game at Madison Square Garden against an NBA All-Star squad," said Pacers assistant coach Vern Fleming. "At a time out, Bobby Knight yelled at us, 'Why don't you go out there and do what he does in practice every day?' Bobby was pointing at Michael."

"Practice is what made Michael go," said Jordan's former coach in Chicago, Doug Collins. "Every day, he had this need to show he was the best. It became part of Michael. Some guys take nights off. Some guys take days off. He never did that. Throw away all the talent. The way he practiced put him on a level above everybody else."

We're at the heart of Jordan now, poking at the purring engine that started him on the path to transcendence. Without the inclination, without the ceaseless work ethic, Jordan is merely another talented athlete gliding through an admirable career, but nothing historic. Without the work ethic, Jordan would have fizzled in his late twenties and flagged in his early thirties, when his natural gifts first began their slow fade, when he was no longer the league's most spectacular athlete, outjumping and outdunking and outrunning everyone.

But Jordan didn't dissolve with age. Just the opposite. He once told Dean Smith that he didn't become a "pure shooter"

> *When I stop working, the rest of the day is posthumous. I'm only really alive when I'm working.*
> —Tennessee Williams
> AUTHOR

until his fourth season in the NBA, and Smith insists that at the final stages of his career, Jordan was as brilliant as he'd ever been, his skills exemplary; in some ways, they were superior to anything they'd ever been. "It frustrates me that his unstinting work ethic is overshadowed by his many other accomplishments," Smith said. "His development was grounded in principles; it wasn't otherworldly, much as he could make it look so."

"I never believed all the press clippings and I never

found comfort in the spotlight," Jordan said. "I don't know how you can and not lose your work ethic. I listened. I was aware of my success, but I never stopped trying to get better."

It doesn't come naturally. No one is born with the inclination toward work. We're born ignorant, our abilities innately undeveloped, our lives lit by distractions. It's easier to watch *The Price Is Right,* to sleep till noon, to procrastinate and postpone until the moment has passed altogether. That's why those who work late, who work dutifully, who implement an intelligent plan, are so often more lauded than those with twice the talent.

"When Michael was in high school, he'd arrive early at school and get the janitor to let him in the gym to shoot," said Wilmington, North Carolina, sportswriter Chuck Caree. "The athletic director would have to run him out of the gym and tell him to go to class."

A study once tracked the careers of a group of elite violinists at the Music Academy of West Berlin. What it revealed is not surprising: By the time the students were eighteen, the best musicians had spent, on average, two thousand more hours in practice than their fellow students.

There is value in repetition, as tedious as it may seem. It's what makes the miraculous seem effortless, what gilds the reputation of our most remarkable athletes.

"Great players never look in the mirror and think, 'I'm a great basketball player,'" Jordan said. "You ask yourself, 'Am I the best player I can be?'"

Pete Maravich would practice his basketball skills for eight hours during the summers as a kid, shooting in steamy hundred-degree gyms, throwing five hundred behind-the-back passes each day, grimacing through quickness and speed drills. Ben Hogan, perhaps the most notoriously relentless worker in the history of golf, would, as a club pro in Pennsylvania, hit 150 balls, play six holes, then go back and hit a few hundred more. Muhammad Ali would run until it hurt, and then keep running, pushing himself into a realm of strength and stamina that most of us never taste. "What counts in the ring," he said, "is what you can do after you're tired." Ted Williams once said, "The key to hitting is just plain working at it. Work, that's the real secret."

> *Being busy does not always mean real work. The object of all work is production and accomplishment and to either of these ends there must be forethought, system, planning, intelligence and honest purpose, as well as perspiration. Seeming to do is not doing.*
> —Thomas Edison

We saw what a fatigued Jordan could do, saw it in the final minutes of games, his bald head shimmering with rivulets of sweat, hands tugging at the ends of his baggy shorts while awaiting a free throw. Dead, then alive, legs lifting off for one last jump shot, body exploding on one final drive toward the basket. That last burst of energy in the final minutes of games was not some divine gift, not an extra wrinkle of Jordan's extraordinary athleticism. This was a premeditated moment, a product of every extended workout. Even when he played baseball, Jordan was the hardest-working player on his team, up at 6:30 A.M. during spring training, arriving in the predawn darkness with hitting coach Walt Hriniak, swinging a bat until his hands tore apart and bled, taping them up and swinging until he bled again.

> *I believe you can accomplish more in forty-five minutes of practice if you work hard than you can in two hours if you don't train properly.*
>
> —Jesse Owens
> OLYMPIC GREAT

"He'd hit early in the afternoon, then take regular batting practice, then hit in the cages before the game and then hit after the game," said Birmingham Barons hitting coach Mike Barnett. "He was starved for information. By August, he'd made himself into a very good hitter."

"I'm not out there sweating for three hours every day," Jordan said, "just to find out what it feels like to sweat."

"He plays as hard—or harder—in practice than he's ever played in games," Jordan's Nike representative, Howard White, once said. "He wants to make the game easier than practice."

That's the other thing about Jordan: Every moment of work led toward an objective. It wasn't just blind labor. It was all part of a grander design.

Michael once observed, "I enjoyed dunking, but I worked much harder on shooting and defense. Again, I know I helped increase the popularity of the dunk and playing above the rim, but I try to practice what I preach. One day I came home and my kids had lowered the basket to nine feet so they could dunk. I raised it back to ten and told them to learn how to shoot."

Jordan began his career with momentous talent. The evidence is in those tapes of him during that first true coming-out party, April 1986, when he poured sixty-three points, a play-off record, onto the Boston Celtics during a double-overtime loss. He took over that game. He split double-teams and floated past defenders, switching the ball from one hand to the other in mid-air. He made nineteen of twenty-one free throws, made twenty-two of forty-one shots from the field, and stunned a Celtics team that was still in the midst of its dynastic form. But look at him, at his narrow frame, twenty-five pounds lighter than it would become, devoid of the pockets of muscle that came to define him in later years. He missed a shot in overtime that would have won the game, a shot that he would not miss in later years. And in the end, despite his efforts, he lost the game, which continued to stand as his overwhelming memory of that night in Boston. He did all he could to prevent that from happening again, sharpening every aspect of his game to the point of treachery.

Jordan began weight training and conditioning a couple of years after that Boston game, after he grew tired of his chief rivals at the time, the Detroit Pistons, constantly wearing him down during games. One summer after the Pistons had won a play-off series against the Bulls, Pistons guard Joe Dumars saw Jordan at a function.

"How long have you been lifting weights?" Jordan said.

"I don't lift," Dumars said. "I run and exercise, but I don't lift."

"I've got to get stronger," Jordan said. "You guys just beat me up too much."

The next season, during a game, Jordan posted up on Dumars down low. Before that, Dumars could have moved Jordan out of position without a problem. But this time, he wouldn't budge.

"He started early, gradually increased his commitment and expanded a program he himself was designing with my help," said Jordan's trainer, Tim Grover.

Soon enough, Jordan had become inured in Grover's regimen, strengthening his upper body while maintaining the elasticity in his legs. He worked on his ankles and his wrists and his shoulders and his knees, all the minute details that would balance his body against the threat of injury. The team would stumble into a hotel on the road at two or three in

> *I do not know anyone who has got to the top without hard work. That is the recipe. It will not always get you to the top, but it should get you pretty near.*
> —Margaret Thatcher

the morning and sometimes Jordan would want to work out then. Other days, when he had exhausted himself during afternoon practices, he would wake up early and be in the gym by 6 A.M., four hours before the team began its regular workouts. (He'd nap briefly in the afternoon.)

Jordan paid for Grover to travel with him. Eventually, he built a home gym, and during his final few years in the league, he would invite teammates Scottie Pippen and Ron Harper over to his house for pre-practice morning workouts. "The Breakfast Club," they called it.

Ron would say, "I'll be there at seven." Michael would say, "6:30." It would always be thirty minutes before what Ron would say. That was MJ saying, "You're going to work a lot harder than you think."

Jordan understood that he was getting older, that his talent alone would not guide him to longevity, that people had built certain expectations about him, that an entire league was laboring to bump him from prominence. So

> *The combination of Michael Jordan's talent and work ethic has never come along.*
> —Steve Kerr

he analyzed himself like an opponent, surveying his own weaknesses, and developing an approach to alleviate them, which is a striking allegory for the mission of any successful life plan.

In seven seasons, with Grover as his trainer, Jordan missed only six games.

"Michael told me the way he kept the crown was always by outworking everyone else," said Seattle Mariners shortstop Alex Rodriguez, who has built a reputation as one of baseball's most diligent young players. "You can always sneak up on people when you're young."

"The challenge," Jordan said late in his career, "is to still do at thirty-five what the young guys are doing at twenty-five or twenty-six."

So this is what happens when the chemicals con-
verge: the talent, the work ethic, the concrete and
foolproof plan commin-

> *Failures are divided into two classes. Those who did and never thought, and those who thought and never did.*
> —John Charles Salak
> WRITER

gling, their cells combin-
ing and multiplying,
forming new elements
and undiscovered com-
pounds, birthing glorious
figures like Jordan, like Pete Maravich and Ben
Hogan, like all of those athletes who ranked a few
notches below the top-ranked Jordan on ESPN's list
of the fifty greatest of the twentieth century.

Those of us immersed in the minutiae of the NBA
have spent the past few seasons combing our ranks
for the "new" Michael Jordan, for someone to replace
the considerable void he left behind after leaving the
game for good. And I can tell you that there is a new
Michael Jordan, someone with his talent, with his
mentality, with his tenacious practice habits. Even has
the same apparel sponsor.

It's just, he plays golf.

"Imagine what would happen if someone with fab-
ulous talent, someone who can hit a golf ball farther
than anyone, who has a swing other pros would kill
to have, was also a grinder," sports author John
Feinstein recently wrote. "Imagine a player who could

be the best in the world without working very hard, who works harder than anyone else.

"That player exists. His name is Tiger Woods, and he is currently dominating golf in ways that seemed impossible before he came along."

"Michael Jordan has adopted Tiger Woods and influenced him greatly," said Greg Boeck of *USA Today*. "As Tiger's mentor, Michael has convinced him that if you want to be the greatest, you have to outwork the opposition every day. You can never let up."

Not long ago, former North Carolina assistant coach Roy Williams played golf with Jordan. They talked about Woods, and Williams asked whether Tiger wouldn't eventually tire of his own success.

> *If there is one characteristic that all great champions share, it's an enormous sense of pride. That's true in all walks of life. The people who excel are those who are driven to show the world ... and prove to themselves ... just how good they are.*
>
> —Nancy Lopez
> PROFESSIONAL GOLFER

"No way, coach," Jordan said. "He's just like me."

Martina Navratilova observed, "At this level talent is a given. But, Tiger works harder than anyone out there, and that's why he's kicking butt. Every great shot you hit, you've already hit a bunch of times in practice."

Another member of the "grinders" school is baseball

Iron Man Cal Ripken. In fact, Cal is the principal. "I've always liked the baseball term 'gamer,'" said Cal. "A gamer to me is someone who comes to the ballpark ready to meet the challenge of the day, every day." Regarding Cal's intense work ethic, his mother Vi said emphatically, "From day one, I've never understood all the hoopla. I mean, isn't this what life is all about—you go out, do a job, come back tomorrow and do it again?"

I have this belief that every soul has a calling, a talent, something that they were born to do, something that was instilled in them at birth. So let's say you've found that talent, and that you work constantly to improve it, to hone its nuances.

That's it. That's how genius is bred.

## Isn't This Fun?

*It's not by doing the things we like, but by liking the things we do that we can discover life's blessings.*

—Goethe

Of course, this all sounds like terrible drudgery, spending hours sweating profusely in a gym, or swinging a baseball bat until the skin on your fingers

> *Do you know why we're so uptight in America? Because the Puritans came here and the really fun people all stayed behind.*
> —Roseanne Barr

begins peeling like a gum wrapper, or—perhaps more realistically—working sixteen-hour days in a cubicle until the numbers begin to perform pirouettes in your cranium. But if this is your calling, your dream, then something happens in the midst of all this labor: Your mind relaxes. You begin to enjoy the routine. And the drudgery is no longer drudgery. And work becomes fun.

Work? Fun?

In America, in our tofu-flavored corporate settings, the previous paragraph has become an oxymoron.

A few years ago my wife and I were in Boston, preparing to run in the Boston Marathon, and we went to see the Red Sox play the Baltimore Orioles. There

> *The appetite to create, is an unbelievable ambition.*
> —Michael Jordan

we encountered a third-base coach named Wendell Kim, a stocky Korean man with chunky legs who would race from the dugout at the end of every half-inning, legs churning, and head bobbing, and scamper back to the dugout after the Red Sox had finished hitting. The Red Sox lost 11–1, and yet we stayed for all nine innings because there remained that fascinating kineticism to Wendell Kim, so anxious to get to his work that he couldn't bear to walk.

The Lakers' Ron Harper said, "Shaquille O'Neal is one of those guys who just loves the game. He's a kid and always will be a kid. He loves to play and to have fun. That's what he's about."

> *Football is game I grew up playing. It was my safe haven, and it was fun and it's a game, and that's the way it has to be. If it stops being fun, you're not going to perform. You're not going to see a bunch of kids out in the park playing if they're not having fun. They're going to do something else.*
> —Mel Renfro
> FORMER NFL PLAYER

I could waste this space citing a dozen studies that reinforce the health benefits of laughter, but I can say the same thing about spinach and you're not going to run to the corner market and buy enough to cram your refrigerator.

> *Give me a man who sings at his work.*
> —Thomas Carlyle

So let me recite this lesson directly, without histrionics or posturing:

Successful people laugh.

Witness: At Southwest Airlines, the *Saturday Night Live* of commercial air travel, flight attendants sing and dance and rap and hide in baggage compartments and hold contests to find the customers with the largest holes in their socks. One of the company's slogans: "We smile because we want to; not because we have to."

"You shouldn't have to change your personality when you come to work," said Southwest CEO Herb Kelleher. "At Southwest we have created an atmos-phere where we hire good people, let them be themselves, and pay a great deal of attention to them and their personal lives."

> *Work can be more fun than fun.*
>
> —Noel Coward
> WRITER

Because of this, Southwest employees are known as the most loyal and productive in the airline industry, and Kelleher has been dubbed "America's Best CEO" by such esteemed judges as the editors of *Fortune* magazine.

Back at the University of North Carolina, at Jordan's alma mater, Dean Smith would sometimes kneel in the middle of the huddle during crucial time-outs, cultivate a wry smile and say, "Isn't this fun?"

And this is another slice of Jordan's allure, that each game was underlaid with an irreverent delight. The tongue dangling loosely from his mouth like an ornament from a rearview mirror. The sheepish grin and shrug of the shoulders captured in the midst of one key play-off game when Jordan seemingly couldn't miss.

"Michael Jordan made up his mind that he's going to enjoy his time playing basketball," said former Bulls assistant coach Tex Winter. "I think he made his mind up a long time ago."

And without the luxury of a single summer break.

# CHAPTER FOUR

# THE FIGHT

**JORDAN ON PERSEVERANCE:**

Obstacles don't have to stop you. If you run into a wall, don't turn around and give up. Figure out how to climb it, go through it or work your way around it.

here would probably be no story here, no moral, no lesson, if Michael Jordan had succumbed to the worst day of his life. It would have trailed off that morning in the tenth grade, when Jordan combed over the varsity cut list at Laney High School in Wilmington, North Carolina. Everyone at Laney had known for weeks the exact day and time that the list would be posted, with the names of those who'd made the roster posted on the wall. Jordan went with his friend Leroy Smith. It was an alphabetical list, and Leroy (who was six feet, eight inches) had made it, and Jordan scanned the Js once, twice. Nothing. He looked at the Ks, at the Hs, at the Is, almost as if he stared for long enough, his name would appear.

That afternoon, after suffering through school, Jordan went home, walked into his room, shut the door so no one could see or hear, and cried. His mother came home from work; he told her he'd been cut, and then cried again. "I told him to go back and discipline himself," his mother recalled. "But I also told

> *Our greatest glory is not in never falling, but in rising every time we fall.*
> —Confucius

him that if he worked hard and still didn't achieve his goal, it just wasn't meant to be."

It was rare for a sophomore to make the varsity at Laney, and Jordan had at least made the junior varsity. Still, it became the sharpest disappointment of Jordan's life. If he had let the sport go, let his aspirations go, none of this would exist. But there was something inside Jordan, something that wouldn't let it be, something that every triumphant individual shares: the ability to look beyond defeat.

## Sticktoitivity

*To endure is greater than to dare. To tire out hostile fortune; to be daunted by no difficulty; to keep heart when all have lost it—who can say this is not greatness?*

—William Makepeace Thackeray
*author*

Here's what Jordan did after he was cut from the

varsity: He played with a possessed aura, with a fire that no one on the jayvee team could contain. The coaches at Laney would say later that they merely cut Jordan from the varsity team because they wanted him to play more. But Jordan didn't see it like that. He saw this as an affront, as a missive. He woke up at six in the morning to shoot around. He practiced in the evenings. Sometimes he scored forty points in jayvee games. The varsity began to show up early to watch him play.

And Jordan wouldn't let the memory of the cut list fade. He refused to be excluded. He volunteered to do anything for the varsity team, even to ride along on the bus to the district tournament. The coaches finally relented. They weren't sure if he could go in the gym with them, so they made him carry the team's uniforms. There was Jordan wending into a gym with a trail of sweatshirts and socks, a task that only made him smolder that much more.

> *Getting cut was good, because it made me know what disappointment felt like, and I knew that I never wanted to have that feeling, ever again . . . that taste in my mouth; that hole in my stomach.*
> —Michael Jordan

Modern America has an obsession with biographies. We watch them on A&E and VH-1 and we browse through them in the expansive biography sections at our local bookstores. Our culture is engrossed with the path of other people's lives, with the contours of their disappointments, their achievements, the moments that shaped them into the people they became. And there's something startlingly similar about these biographies, one common theme, one shared image. There is always a moment in every one in which our hero could have quit, could have abandoned his passion, his drive, his yearning, and meandered on to something else.

And the catch, of course, is that if they had, there would be no biography.

This next story is fitting, then, since we've already touched on the similarities between Jordan and Bill Russell, the way they approached basketball with the same sort of tireless perfectionism. Bill Russell, too, was cut from his high school basketball team, from the junior varsity. And Russell had the same emotions

> *During Michael's sophomore year at UNC, they played against Virginia and Ralph Sampson. UNC trailed by twelve with three or four minutes to go when MJ took over. He made steals, hit big shots. It was like, "World look out, here I come." George Brett once told me that when he was driving to hit .400 one season the thing that pushed him was the fear that he was never going to get a hit again. I think MJ had some of that.*
>
> —Larry Donald
> BASKETBALL WRITER

when he saw the cut list at McClymonds High School in Oakland, California, when he scanned it and couldn't find his name. He stared for what seemed like an hour, thinking, like Jordan, that if he looked long enough, his name would appear. "That," Russell said, "was one of the most devastating things that ever happened to me."

So it is not coincidence that Jordan and Russell both developed that same prickly exterior, the same fierce ambition. For both, it began with the first letdown. With the cut. With the realization that failure could happen to them.

### Study by a National Retail Association

*48 percent of all salesmen make one call and stop.*

*25 percent of all salesmen make two calls and stop.*

*15 percent of all salesmen make three calls and stop.*

*12 percent of all salesmen go back continuously. These salesmen make 80 percent of all sales.*

> *Sometimes, I found myself thinking that, if Michael hadn't been cut from the team . . . if he hadn't been sent away . . . he might never have become who he is.*
>
> —Bob Greene
> COLUMNIST

It's easy enough to give in. There are scientific studies that reveal the power of surrender—surveys of rats who have been held in hand so firmly that there is no possibility of escape, or put in a tank of water and mandated to swim to safety. Eventually they give in. They succumb to the virtual impossibility of the odds.

The numbers go like this, according to one university professor: Most businesspeople fail approximately 3.8 times before they find success. And there are stories to perpetuate that claim, well-documented tales of successful humans' dalliances with defeat.

Edison experimented with two thousand materials before discovering the correct type for a light-bulb filament. Walt Disney was fired from a newspaper for possessing a "lack of ideas." (In researching a book I wrote about Disney, called *Go for the Magic*, I discovered that he'd formulated his own term for persistence. "Sticktoitivity," Disney called it, and I figure that works as well as anything.) Leo Tolstoy flunked out of college. Woody Allen flunked motion-picture production. Lucille Ball had a producer advise her to get out of acting, to "Try any other profession. Any other." The Beatles were turned away from a record-label audition, Buddy Holly was fired from his label and Bob Dylan was booed from the stage of a high school talent show. Vince Lombardi didn't become an NFL coach until he turned forty-seven. Chuck Daly had no head coaching success in the NBA until he was fifty-two.

> *History has demonstrated that the most notable winners usually encountered heartbreaking obstacles before they triumphed. They won because they refused to become discouraged by their defeats.*
> —B. C. Forbes
> AUTHOR

This comes from one of Jordan's myriad shoe advertisements, but it seems to nestle nicely into this chapter:

"I've missed more than nine thousand shots in my career. I've lost almost three hundred games. Twenty-six times, I've been trusted to take the game-winning shot and missed. I've failed over and over and over again in my life, and that is why I succeed."

"One day, MJ and I were set to play golf in Chicago," said former NFL wide receiver Erick Martin. "We teed off at 9 A.M., and it was raining. We ended up playing forty-five holes in the rain. MJ said, 'If we start, we're going to finish.'"

"One day we played golf with Davis Love III," said

Jordan's former college roommate, Buzz Peterson. "Michael knew he couldn't beat him, so his goal was to outdrive him on just one hole. I think we played forty-five holes. Michael never did do it, but he was not going to stop trying."

"During those great series between the New York Knicks and Chicago, New York had the better team," said former Knicks guard Mark Jackson. "We broke the Bulls' will. But MJ single-handedly won the series for Chicago. He would not allow them to surrender."

"Some people get frozen by a fear of failure," Jordan said. "They get it from their peers or from just thinking about the possibility of negative results. They might be afraid of looking bad or being embarrassed. I realized that if I was going to achieve anything in life, I had to be aggressive. I had to get out there and go for it."

> There wouldn't be any sneakers named after Michael Jordan if he had given up in high school.
> —Derek Jeter
> New York Yankees' Shortstop

Some of the healthiest examples of persistence in our society come in the form of cartoon characters. Who among us can't relate to the everlasting will of Charlie Brown, who for years attempted to kick the same football, to pitch the same baseball, to date the same little red-haired girl? Or to Wile E. Coyote, who continually endangers his physical well-being for the sake of capturing the same elusive Road Runner?

These characters became cultural icons because there are pieces of each in all of us, because there is no one who hasn't failed, who hasn't felt like everything they tried was colored in futility, that there was nothing to look forward to except continual frustration. But these are also characters born of hope, fueled by the value of persistence.

"He keeps trying, over and over and over," said Wile E. Coyote creator Chuck Jones. "That trait is possibly the only thing that all creative people have in common. They don't give up."

"There is one thing I learned a long time ago," said *Peanuts* and Charlie Brown creator Charles Schulz. "If you can hang on for a while longer,

> *The man who can drive himself further once the effort gets painful, is the man who will win."*
> —Roger Bannister
> FIRST TO RUN A MILE
> IN LESS THAN FOUR MINUTES

there is always something bright around the corner. The dark clouds will go away and there will be some sunshine again if you're able to hold out. I think you just have to wait it out."

It was no great secret what would happen in the fourth quarter of a taut game in Jordan's realm. It was as if the rest of the court faded to black and white and Jordan remained, taking the ball, driving to the hoop, getting knocked down hard, drawing a foul, over and over and over again, until it became almost comical. The opposing team could try anything, could knock him down in brutal fashion, and he'd continue to rise and try it again. Eventually, they'd wear down. Jordan wouldn't. He could be sick. He could be exhausted, clinging to his shorts, tongue draped from his mouth, and he'd keep driving, keep getting battered, keep shooting foul shots into eternity.

> *Nothing in the world can take the place of persistence. Talent will not; nothing is more common than unsuccessful men with talent. Genius will not; unrewarded genius is almost a proverb. Education will not; the world is full of educated derelicts. Persistence and determination alone are omnipotent.*
> —Calvin Coolidge

"When I was with the Nuggets, we were up on the Bulls in Denver by twenty-six in the fourth quarter," said former NBA player Danny Schayes. "We hung on to win by three. Michael got fifty-two. He was incredible. We were lucky to hang on. He never quit in the fourth quarter. No lead was safe with Michael in the game."

"MJ would keep driving to the hole time after time," said former NBA player Xavier McDaniel. "You hit him and knock him down; most guys would start to pull up and take jump shots. Not MJ. He'd never stop going to the rack, no matter how many times you knocked him down."

"With Michael Jordan you could never let your guard down," said former NBA guard Paul Pressey. "He was so relentless you couldn't rest for a second because he was always on the attack, always dogging you. And he did it on the bench, too. He'd study everything and when he'd get back in the game he'd have picked something up to attack you more."

Mark Randall, a former Bulls player, recalled: "One year in an exhibition game, we were losing badly late in the game. During a time-out, MJ yelled at all of us 'Don't ever think about quitting tonight. If they think you're weak now, then later in the season they'll kill you when it counts.'"

My adopted son David spent two weeks in college before deciding it wasn't for him. The next day, I took him straight to the Marine recruiting station; let's just say that he enrolled voluntarily, but if he wasn't going to finish

> *Fight one more round. When your feet are so tired that you have to shuffle back to the center of the ring, fight one more round. When your arms are so tired that you can hardly lift your hands to come on guard, fight one more round. When your nose is bleeding and your eyes are black and you are so tired that you wish your opponent would crack you one on the jaw and put you to sleep, fight one more round—remember that the man who always fights one more round is never whipped.*
>
> —James J. Corbett
> HEAVYWEIGHT BOXER

college, he didn't have a whole lot of choice. He went through twelve weeks of basic training at Parris Island, South Carolina, with no contact from the outside world. The next time we saw him was at his graduation ceremony. Afterward, the Marines were released to their parents, who waited out on the tarmac.

When David saw me, he began to cry. He threw his arms around me and buried his head in my shoulder.

"I heard your voice the whole time, Dad," he said. "I didn't quit."

There is obviously a pathway to persistence. It relates heavily to the Jordan we've already discussed, to the man who pushed himself harder than anyone in the game, who disciplined himself with almost alarming harshness.

The pathway to persistence lies in self-discipline.

# The Soul of an Army

*Being a professional, is doing all the things you love to do on the days you don't feel like doing them.*

—Julius Erving

It was at North Carolina that Jordan first honed his sense of discipline. Here again, it was Dean Smith who influenced him, who led him to the realization that nothing is accomplished without the ability to push through hardships, to deny small yearnings for the sake of the greater goal.

"I believe that the disciplined guy can do anything," Smith said. "He can choose to stay up late or not. He can choose to smoke ten packs of cigarettes or not. Usually, the people coming into college basketball had to have some discipline, or they wouldn't be that good. They've had to say no a lot of times to other things to go work on their basketball. And players still want to be disciplined. They feel loved when they're disciplined."

"One day at practice, Dean Smith read a 'Thought of the Day'," said former North Carolina trainer Mark Davis. "The quote was 'Discipline makes you free.' MJ was there. He heard it. I think that quote captures him."

> *Discipline is the soul of an army. It makes small numbers formidable, procures success to the weak and esteem to all.*
> —George Washington

One of my all-time favorite movies is *Lean on Me,* a story about principal Joe Clark trying to resurrect an inner-city high school in Newark, New Jersey. Clark, played by Morgan Freeman, utters this classic line: "Discipline is not the enemy of enthusiasm."

In 1975, Junko Tabei became the first female to climb Mount Everest. After her success she said, "Technique and ability alone do not get you to the top; it is the willpower that is the most important—it rises in your heart."

There are those moments when no one is watching, those times when work becomes laborious, when we feel as if we're going to sink underneath our desks, when we wish we could go home and sleep for months at a time. We live large portions of life like this, in that period athletes call The Grind. And I have noticed that this is the period of life in which most people tend to throw up their arms and surrender. But this is when the victorious figures of our society have done the opposite. They've developed an immunity to The Grind. "The Grind," said ex-tennis star Jimmy Connors, "is the stew of talent and determination that keeps certain players hammering on, even when the match score favors the opponent. The Grind is the sweat addiction that pulls some players out of bed in spite of aches and muscle strains. It's the part of all this I enjoy the most."

Jordan thrived in The Grind, in those times when

his natural instincts wouldn't have led him to a basketball court, when he had to fight his mind and his body, grit through pain and doubt just to make it onto the court. That ability to persevere, to grind even at his weakest, is a product of strength, of will, of preparation, most of it within the walls of his own psyche. It's the product of Jordan continually pushing himself to untold limits.

Stacey King, one of Michael's teammates in Chicago, offers a revealing insight: "MJ's special strength was his ability to play through pain. He just blocked out the pain of a sprained ankle or foot injury and wouldn't miss a game. Most guys would be out for two weeks, but not MJ. His focus and mental toughness were awesome. (Allen Iverson shows glimpses of that now, but he's about the only one like Mike that way.) The result was that MJ forced his teammates to play up to his level because he came to every practice and game ready to go all out. People see the glitz and glamour of MJ's life, but they didn't see the hard work, preparation and pain he went through."

He played in Phoenix with an infected foot. The Suns' team doctor wanted him to go home. Jordan refused. Instead, he played every night on that road trip.

He played once with a broken cheekbone, with blood leaking into his sinus cavity. He never missed a game. He never even missed a practice. He never used a facemask.

"One day, Michael had back spasms in his lower back so bad, we had to carry him off the bus," said Phil Jackson. "He got forty that night."

The Bulls' team doctor, John Hefferon, would often see Jordan's father, and James Jordan would ask how his son was feeling, and Hefferon would say he wasn't feeling well, that the flu was coming on, that his stomach was upset. "That mean's Michael's going to have a great game tonight," James Jordan would say.

And most of the time, he was right.

This story comes from a man named Marty Dim. He and his fifteen-year-old son were playing golf at Briarwood Country Club in Chicago one afternoon, and when they reached the fourth tee, they caught up with Michael Jordan, who invited them to play the rest of the course with him. Dim's son was so nervous he could barely speak.

> *Do something every day that you don't want to do. This is the golden rule for acquiring the habit of doing your duty without pain.*
> —Mark Twain

On the fifth hole, Jordan hit his drive into a bush. He hacked out, emerging with torn clothes and scratches on his arm, and made par.

On the sixth green, Dim's son was still a wreck. He

lagged behind. He saw that the others were finished playing and told them to go ahead.

Jordan was on the far side of the green. He charged across, stopped a few inches from the kid's face, and said, "Are you quitting on me?" He repeated it, over and over. "Are you quitting on me? Are you quitting on me?"

"Michael," Marty Dim said, "just would not let him give up."

> *In the 1989 Chicago-Detroit play-offs, I saw a play that I think was the defining moment of Michael's career. He drove down the middle and Rick Mahorn and Bill Laimbeer hammered him to the ground. Hard. He got up limping. The next game, he was still banged up. That was Michael tasting the NBA at its most bitter. After that, he realized he had to take over.*
>
> —Mike Abdenour
> TRAINER, DETROIT PISTONS

Which leads us back to Game Five of those 1997 NBA Finals, Jordan fighting a vengeful flu virus and taking intravenous fluids, his pallor so gray that one sportswriter said he literally "shook with fear" for him. And when Mike Wise of the *New York Times* surveyed Jordan's gaunt figure late in the game, he leaned over press row and muttered to Michael Wilbon of the *Washington Post,* "It's over." Wise did what many print reporters fighting deadline had done. He wrote his story as if Utah had won the game. And while he was writing, Jordan—as if once again summoned by adversity—began to alter the course of Wise's story single-handedly, to scrape through the debilitation and win this game virtually by himself. And to demonstrate, Wise said, "what perseverance really is."

But this perseverance was not merely a lone act of will. It was a build-up, the summation of years of training, of Jordan sharpening his own resolution. And eventually developing an impenetrable wall of discipline.

> *Once you learn to quit it becomes a habit.*
> —Vince Lombardi

"His body wouldn't let him down at the moment of truth because of the way he had trained it," said *Chicago Tribune* columnist Bernie Lincicome. "It didn't know how to quit."

# CHAPTER FIVE

# THE PROMISE

**JORDAN ON RESPONSIBILITY:**

The game is my wife. It demands loyalty and responsibility, and it gives me back fulfillment and peace.

# READER/CUSTOMER CARE SURVEY

We care about your opinions! Please take a moment to fill out our online Reader Survey at **http://survey.hcibooks.com.**

As a **"THANK YOU"** you will receive a **VALUABLE INSTANT COUPON** towards future book purchases

as well as a **SPECIAL GIFT** available only online! Or, you may mail this card back to us.

(PLEASE PRINT IN ALL CAPS)

First Name _____ MI. _____ Last Name _____

Address _____ City _____

State _____ Zip _____ Email _____

**1. Gender**
- ❑ Female
- ❑ Male

**2. Age**
- ❑ 8 or younger
- ❑ 9-12
- ❑ 13-16
- ❑ 17-20
- ❑ 21-30
- ❑ 31+

**3. Did you receive this book as a gift?**
- ❑ Yes
- ❑ No

**4. Annual Household Income**
- ❑ under $25,000
- ❑ $25,000 - $34,999
- ❑ $35,000 - $49,999
- ❑ $50,000 - $74,999
- ❑ over $75,000

**5. What are the ages of the children living in your house?**
- ❑ 0 - 14
- ❑ 15+

**6. Marital Status**
- ❑ Single
- ❑ Married
- ❑ Divorced
- ❑ Widowed

**7. How did you find out about the book?**
*(please choose one)*
- ❑ Recommendation
- ❑ Store Display
- ❑ Online
- ❑ Catalog/Mailing
- ❑ Interview/Review

**8. Where do you usually buy books?**
*(please choose one)*
- ❑ Bookstore
- ❑ Online
- ❑ Book Club/Mail Order
- ❑ Price Club (Sam's Club, Costco's, etc.)
- ❑ Retail Store (Target, Wal-Mart, etc.)

**9. What subject do you enjoy reading about the most?**
*(please choose one)*
- ❑ Parenting/Family
- ❑ Relationships
- ❑ Recovery/Addictions
- ❑ Health/Nutrition
- ❑ Christianity
- ❑ Spirituality/Inspiration
- ❑ Business Self-help
- ❑ Women's Issues
- ❑ Sports

**10. What attracts you most to a book?**
*(please choose one)*
- ❑ Title
- ❑ Cover Design
- ❑ Author
- ❑ Content

TAPE IN MIDDLE; DO NOT STAPLE

# BUSINESS REPLY MAIL
FIRST-CLASS MAIL  PERMIT NO 45  DEERFIELD BEACH, FL

POSTAGE WILL BE PAID BY ADDRESSEE

Health Communications, Inc.
3201 SW 15th Street
Deerfield Beach FL 33442-9875

FOLD HERE

Comments

*The price of greatness is responsibility.*
—Winston Churchill

I am what some would call an old-fashioned father. To my children, this means I'm mired in a black-and-white pre–*Leave It to Beaver* utopia, in a mentality that is so removed from their own consciousness, they have trouble believing the human race existed back then. Mostly, my children think that I belong in the 1940s. Sometimes, if they are feeling generous, they will inform me that I have advanced to the 1950s, but still they consider me marooned in an Eisenhower-era dream world.

I also know that most of the time, my children are correct. Take the trend of body piercing and permanent tattoos, something that I encounter every day as an NBA executive. Regarding tattoos, this is my rule with my children: As long as they are living under my roof, eating meals and wearing clothes that are paid for with my salary, they will get no tattoos, and they will not pierce anything that could not be exposed in church.

Strict, perhaps. But I am not an ogre. I offer one exception to the rule. Each child is allowed one tattoo. The caveat is that I choose the location and the design of the tattoo. The location I would choose is the forehead. The design I would choose is a bold proclamation: "I AM IN CHARGE OF ME!" Not only will I pay for this procedure, but I will provide a substantial signing bonus. And yet, astoundingly, none of my children has taken me up on this.

The offer still stands.

> *Michael Jordan was looked at as a savior to lead 35 million African Americans out of the wilderness. That's a huge responsibility. MJ takes a lot of abuse for what he hasn't done socially, but don't forget, he's an athlete, not an activist. He's done so much for people that we'll never hear about. He takes a lot of flack, but he's always there.*
> —Spike Lee
> FILMMAKER

This goes back to Game Six again, to Jordan's magnum opus, his last shot against Utah in 1998. But it also goes back to every shot he took in the final minutes, every one of those times he took the weight of a game and a season and a franchise upon his shoulders. It got to the point where no one had a question who would take the shot, or who would accept the brunt of the responsibility for a defeat. Jordan depended on his teammates, but more than anything, he depended on himself, on his willingness to look past defeat in order to deliver victory the next time. "You must give the other guys an opportunity to shine," he said of his teammates. "But at the same time, my philosophy has always been that if I'm going to go down, I want to go down shooting."

"In training camp in 1995, a bunch of us were in the training room after practice," said former Bulls center Bill Wennington, "and Michael said to us, 'You guys better jump on

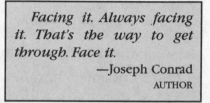

*Facing it. Always facing it. That's the way to get through. Face it.*
—Joseph Conrad
AUTHOR

my back and hold on for your life, because if you fall off, you're not going all the way. It's going to be a bumpy ride, but I'm going to do it.'"

This is a touchy subject we've delved into, that of responsibility. We live in a world of frivolous lawsuits, of immense deflection of liability. There is a void of culpability, of people willing to admit their mistakes in a public forum (See our former President, for one). Those who do wrong can now hide behind lawyers and publicists, and deflect blame to the circumstances or the media or their state of mind, to anything but themselves. We are a nation marred by childish acts. Not so with Michael Jordan

"If you tell Michael, 'Bad shot,' he says, 'Yes,' and he doesn't argue," said Phil Jackson. "He'll take a shot and say, 'I messed up. I probably shouldn't have taken that shot.'"

All of which leads me back to my own flock of children.

See, despite being a man mired deep in the past, I like to consider myself a student of various aspects of human nature. One of

> Difficulty is the excuse
> history never accepts.
> —Edward R. Murrow

these is the Art of the Excuse. I have a daughter—she shall go unnamed here—who virtually mutilated the eleventh grade at her Orlando high school. I believe the entire school is still undergoing therapy. In the midst of this, I tried futilely to deliver nightly sermons to my daughter about her poor school work, about the immense effect it could have upon her future. Finally, after she came home having done something so terrible that I can't even remember it, I lost myself altogether. "That's it," I said to her. "I have to know what's going on."

"It's not my fault that the teachers don't know how to teach me right," she said.

I proceeded to implode, right there at the kitchen table.

I had another daughter in the eighth grade who, according to reports, was a continual disruption in her classroom. So I demanded an explanation.

"It's not my fault that the teacher puts me next to a boy who makes me laugh," she said.

Another of my daughters, who had good grades in all of her classes except biology, once insisted that her biology teacher was bent on "messing up my grade-point average."

But I'm not finished. There is a footnote to the story from the Mexican restaurant I shared a couple of chapters ago, the story of my two boys and their dramatic tales of burnout. Even after my son Thomas announced that the schoolwork was too much for him, he continued to hide behind excuses. This is what he told me:

> *Some people spend their entire lives thinking they are where they are because of circumstances. You are not what you are because of where you were born or who your parents are.*
> —Roger Dawson
> AUTHOR

"It's not my fault that I'm writing papers that are over the professor's head."

And with that, I nearly coughed up my taco.

\* \* \*

Jordan was drafted by one of the NBA's lowliest franchises. The Chicago Bulls were a laughingstock when he joined them, a losing team playing in a crumbling stadium with virtually no tradition. He could have signed a short-term contract and skipped town when the team continued to struggle. Instead,

> *One of the annoying things about believing in free choice and individual responsibility is the difficulty of finding somebody to blame your problems on. And when you do find somebody, it's remarkable how often his picture turns up on your driver's license.*
> —P. J. O'Rourke
> WRITER

he elevated the franchise to an unprecedented height. He changed everything. Now the Bulls are one of the NBA's most recognizable franchises— even without Jordan— because Jordan felt an obligation to nurture the team that drafted him. "Part of the responsibility which went with your contract was to turn that team around and make it a winner—in fact, make it a champion," said former Celtics coach Chris Ford. "That was an obligation, and it was deeply felt. I'm afraid not a lot of people feel that way today."

It's also why Jordan never left the Bulls to play elsewhere during their championship run, even when his relationship with the team's management became strained, even when seemingly everything he could have achieved was behind him. "I was the nucleus of the franchise when I came here and we went through the process of going from bad to good," Jordan said. "I have a certain responsibility to this franchise and to the city of Chicago."

Bill Guthridge inherited the North Carolina basketball program in 1997 after Jordan's coach, Dean Smith, finally retired. And yet Smith's aura still hung over the Carolina basketball office, in the spirit of the "Excuse Jar" on Guthridge's desk, in which those who came to see him were expected to file their excuses before they began talking.

> *When I played for Sacramento, I blocked Michael's shot with eight seconds left and we won the game. After the game, Michael told the writers he had no excuses. He gave me credit for a good play. He said, "We didn't get it done." I never forgot that.*
>
> —LaSalle Thompson
> FORMER NBA PLAYER

So what are we responsible for in our everyday lives? Simple. We're responsible for what we do, for what we say, for the way we carry ourselves, for the way we spend our time, for the way we think and act and associate with others. We are responsible for everything that encompasses us, and everything that belongs to us.

Oprah Winfrey hit it on the head when she wrote, "We are each responsible for our own life—no other person is or ever can be."

# Broccoli and Bookstores

Mostly, we are responsible for ourselves, which is one of those blanket statements that carries only a vague definition on the surface. Because really, what

> *A balanced meal is not a Big Mac in both hands.*
> —Ken Hussar
> HUMORIST

does it mean to be responsible for ourselves? It means we take care of ourselves. It means we strive to improve, both the mental definition and physical definition of self. It means we expand our minds at every opportunity and we take meticulous care of our body before it begins to malfunction. At its core, it means two things: our education and our health. Both are continuous processes. In fact, I'm still convinced that one of the best investments we can make in ourselves is a pair of running shoes, a comfortable T-shirt and pair of shorts, and, if you prefer, a headband. From there, you can take it any direction: Buy a used Stairmaster at a yard sale. Walk through the neighborhood each afternoon. It's not like you have to undertake the Michael Jordan workout plan and attempt to melt away all of your body fat; it is a small commitment that pays immense dividends.

Aerobic guru Dr. Ken Cooper makes it very simple:

If you walk two miles in thirty minutes three times a week, or two miles in forty minutes five times a week, you will have a 58 percent reduction in death by heart attack, stroke or cancer and increase your life span up to six years. Marathoner Grete Waitz was right

> *One day during the 1997-98 season, Phil Jackson called off a practice. Michael said to Scottie Pippen, "We're not playing well enough not to practice." So they went to Phil and requested a practice. Turned out they practiced for three hours. Later, MJ said, "The best players have to be the caretakers."*
>
> —Michael Wilbon
> SPORTSWRITER

when she stated, "Life is movement. It's the person who sits on the couch—they're living dangerously."

It is the easiest of our responsibilities to understand, and yet, amid a nation laden with greasy burgers and double-chocolate fudge sundaes with extra whipped cream, it is the most ignored. So let me say this directly: if you subsist on Whoppers and Big Macs and the double-pepperoni special, and if you wind up with high cholesterol and blocked arteries, it is YOUR FAULT. If you smoke for thirty years and don't make the effort to quit, and you wind up with lung cancer, it is YOUR FAULT.

I don't want to turn this into a Dr. Atkins book, but I know enough to tell you that small balanced meals are more effective than lumberjack breakfasts and large unwieldy dinners, that bright vegetables contain

> *It's a burden to be good every night. A lot of guys want to be good, but they don't want the responsibility day-to-day.*
> —Mike Thibault
> NBA ASSISTANT COACH

more vitamins than dark chocolates, and that Twinkies are not a food group.

I also know it does not take much. My mother is now in her late eighties, and has done absolutely nothing sensible about her health in her entire life. My sisters and I have developed this theory, then, that the only thing keeping her alive is the one healthy food she does eat: broccoli. Of course, she smothers the broccoli in mayonnaise, or in cheese sauce, but she does eats it, and as I write this, she's still living well.

We have already explored Jordan's propensity for learning new things, for submitting to the tutelage of men like Dean Smith, like Kevin Loughery, like Phil Jackson. It is, obviously, a slightly different sort of learning than what typical humans—those of us with flat jump shots and a four-inch vertical leap—must submit ourselves to; and yet the learning process is the same.

> *I am always ready to learn, although I do not always like being taught.*
> —Winston Churchill

We pay attention; we study; we question what we don't understand; we apply ourselves to the problem until we do understand. We accomplish everything that my college-aged sons seem determined to avoid. Our reward is esoteric, but it is also an immense compensation: greater recognition, greater comprehension, greater intelligence and a greater chance of approaching Jordan-esque levels of success.

"The four laws of learning are explanation, demonstration, imitation and repetition," said legendary college basketball coach John Wooden. "The goal is to create a correct habit that can be produced instinctively under great pressure. To make sure this goal was achieved, I created eight laws of learning—namely, explanation, demonstration, imitation, repetition, repetition, repetition, repetition and repetition."

"I should never stop learning," Jordan said. "I just want to keep learning about everything I can ... about my life, about my family and about me. It can all end so quickly. You don't know when. So you've got to give yourself every experience, because if you don't, you may never get the chance."

Wizards co-owner Ted Leonsis said "Michael is a serious student in the high-tech world and is always learning how to use the latest gadgets. He's a quick study."

Not long ago, I got a phone call from my son Bobby, who was in graduate school at the time, and has since begun his career as a coach in the Cincinnati Reds

> *On my epitaph I want it written, "He was curious to the end."*
> —Tom Peters
> SPEAKER AND AUTHOR

farm system. I've tried to impart whatever wisdom I might still have rattling around in my cranium (I'm an old man, remember). But you never know how successful you've been with your children. You're never sure what they might have learned, which is why this phone call nearly gave me chills.

"Dad," Bobby said. "I've got a goal."

I asked him what it was.

"Ten books," he said. "I want to read ten books by Christmas."

"You mean you have to read ten books by Christmas," I said, "for school."

"No," he said. "I want to read ten books for Christmas—outside of school."

One of the first books I read after graduating from college altered the course of my life. *Veeck: As in Wreck,* the autobiography of a chain-smoking one-legged baseball owner named Bill Veeck, was intelligent and insightful and bold and hilarious and written in the wonderful cadence of a man who attacked life like none I'd known. I called Veeck soon after I read it, and I visited him at his home in Maryland, and eventually he became my mentor, guiding me through the early stages of my career as a minor-league baseball executive.

I mention Veeck because I mention reading, and the first person I think of when I wander into a used bookstore, meandering through shelves crammed with volumes of poetry and biographics and heavy first editions of novels, is Veeck. He read four or five books a week. He read while soaking the stump of his amputated leg (he lost it in World War II) every morning. He read in every spare moment. I've tried to emulate it, to the point where my wife Ruth once accused me of reading too much.

> *When I get a little money, I buy books. And if any is left, I buy food and clothes.*
> —Erasmus

Bill believed that "With a book, you can be anything you want. With TV, you watch what someone pre-determines you should watch. You can be anything with a book. You can be in any part of the world. You can be with Marco Polo in China. The next day you can be in the South Sea islands with Melville. You can be Tom Sawyer or Huck Finn on a raft. No other way can you find that ability to be so many different people in so many different places."

I cannot emphasize this point enough. Our society constantly attempts to determine the reason for the degeneration of its youth's knowledge. The answer is

> *Old men are always advising young men to save money. That is bad advice. Don't save every nickel. Invest in yourself. I never saved a dollar until I was forty years old.*
> —Henry Ford

wrapped in the printed word, in an entire generation of readers who have been swallowed by television. A statistic: If you finish this book, and if you read one more book each month for the next year, you are among the top 1 percent of intellectuals in America.

It is such a simple step toward self-improvement, and yet so few people carve out the time to do it. Football coach John McKay tried to read one book a day. Wow!

# The Chain of Responsibility

Certainly there is another layer of responsibility beyond just our education and our health, the literal halves of ourselves. Once we have begun to acquire understanding and knowledge, we are accountable for the ways in which we utilize them. Here's what I'm talking about:

# Attitude
# (or, the Way We Think)

I grew up idolizing St. Louis Cardinals icon Stan Musial, and today I cannot think of him without recalling a story from St. Louis sportswriter Bob Broeg about Musial's playing days. One day, Broeg recalls, a Cardinals player nearly skipped into the clubhouse, bubbling with enthusiasm. He burbled, "I feel great! My home life is happy. I'm in a groove. I feel like I'm going to get two hits today."

> *Product and price can be attractive to customers. But your attitude is what brings them back or drives them away.*
>
> —Mark Holmes
> SPEAKER

He turned to Musial. He said, "Ever feel that way, Stan?"

"Every day," Musial said.

Roger Bannister broke one of humankind's seemingly impassable barriers when he ran a sub-four-minute mile in 1954; it was a feat preceded by months of excruciating physical practice. But there was more to it than that. In order to shatter the boundaries, he had to visualize shattering the boundaries. And so he imagined his run, all of it, every stride, every turn, every second from start to finish.

A year after Bannister's run, thirty-seven people

broke the barrier, and within another year, three hundred more had done it. Today it is commonplace, but it was Bannister's run that gave them the strength, the ability, the belief.

"My mother," Michael Jordan said, "planted the belief that the ability to achieve starts in your mind."

Football coach Bill Walsh said, "It's almost a serene, purist state of mind you get in when you're competing with full, ultimate confidence, poise, self-assurance and preparation. "It's the negatives that you don't want to cross your mind; the apprehension about whether you're good enough, whether you're prepared, or the fear that your opponent is simply better than you are. You must train yourself to cut through all that."

Our thinking can restrain us. Or it can power us forward.

# Words
# (or, the Way We Talk)

There is a certain responsibility in being thrust into the public spotlight. Your words are scrutinized. You have to be very careful. You have to watch your mouth, control your voice, stem your emotion. This is

> *The best of conversations occur when there is no competition, no vanity, but a calm, quiet interchange of sentiments.*
> —Samuel Johnson
> WRITER

something Jordan did with a meticulousness that belied his status. Few people were more studied or more well-attended by media—not even some world leaders—and yet Jordan never allowed himself to make a blatant slip, to let anger or frustration overcome him.

We are not facing the same universal pressures as Jordan, but there's no reason why our expectations for ourselves shouldn't be just as stringent. Words define us. Sometimes we say things we shouldn't. There are those rare moments when we can't restrain it. But what we can help is how often we let it happen, and how we control our language amid the routine of our daily lives. This is our responsibility.

# Hearing
# (or, the Way We Listen)

*It is the disease of not listening, the malady of not marking, that I am troubled withal.*

—William Shakespeare

There is no use even bothering with conversation if we are only preoccupied with our own concerns. The problem is that most of us don't utilize conversation the way we should—to absorb and consider the knowledge and viewpoint of others. Instead, we filter everything through the lens of our own concerns, we worry about formulating an appropriate reply and we don't really listen.

> I knew Michael Jordan was unusual from the second day of practice his freshman year. I was teaching some pressure defense principles and saw Michael was doing it incorrectly. I went over it with him. I thought it would take him two weeks to learn it. The next day, Michael had it down perfectly. I said, "What did you do, stay up all night studying?" He said, "Coach, I'm a good listener. I do what I'm supposed to do."
> —Dean Smith

The average person can speak about 150 words per minute; we are able, if we hone our listening skills, to hear as many as 600 words per minute. It is a way to build trust and self-esteem in our relationships. It is a way to build our own self-defense.

Former Secretary of State Dean Rusk stated, "One of the best ways to persuade others is with your ears—by listening to them."

Some simple solutions for listening more effectively, borrowed from *Listening in Everyday Life,* by Michael Purdy and Deborah Borisoff are:

**Keep quiet.** It signals your receptiveness.

**Don't lead.** Asking leading questions is a way of directing the conversation.

**Resist giving advice unless they ask directly.** Often, people are not searching for solutions to their problems; they just want someone to engage them.

**Remain neutral.** Don't agree or disagree, approve or disapprove.

**Don't react defensively.** If you hear something that bothers you, avoid showing it.

**Avoid clichés.** This only leads people to think you're anxious to get away from them.

# Friends (or, the Way We Build Relationships)

*Friendship is the hardest thing in the world to explain. It's not something you learn in school, but if you haven't learned the meaning of friendship, you haven't really learned anything.*

—Muhammad Ali

Perhaps it isn't something we think about often, but we are responsible for the friends we choose. Sometimes friends fall into our lives. Sometimes they fall out. It is our responsibility to encircle ourselves with friends who enrich us, who encourage us, who boost us, who help us believe that our goals will become reality. Which leads me to the story of the monkeys. Although it's not a story, really. It's an experiment in friendship.

Four monkeys were placed in a room with a tall pole in the center and a cluster of bananas suspended at the top of the pole. One of the monkeys began climbing the pole. He was doused with cold water as he reached for the banana. He scampered down the pole and abandoned the bananas. The other three monkeys also tried—they were doused, they scampered down and they gave up.

> *Keep away from people who try to belittle your ambitions. Small people always do that, but the really great make you feel that you, too, can become great.*
> —Mark Twain

One of the monkeys was removed from the room and replaced with a new monkey. He began to climb the pole. The other three monkeys tugged at him, scraped at him, pulled him to the ground. One by one, each of the original monkeys was replaced, until there were four monkeys in a room, dancing around the pole, afraid to climb, even though none of them knew why.

Author Danny Cox writes, "Don't walk away from negative people—run!"

It speaks loudly that Jordan, despite his immense fame, never became immersed in the tragic saga of so many modern athletes: the tug and pull of pseudo-friendships, of those who are determined to use the skills and assets of others to accomplish their own needs. This is what led to the downfall of Sammie Smith, the former Miami Dolphins running back who was jailed for dealing cocaine.

"I didn't need the money," Smith said. "These were my friends, and I just couldn't turn my back on them. We saw an easy way to make money."

# Minutiae (or, the Way We Deal with the Little Things)

*Always check the small things.*
—General Colin Powell

The best athletes are attuned to the tiniest facets of their game, to the specks of detail that delineate success and failure. Not long ago the Ted Williams Museum bought a bat that a collector had paid twenty thousand dollars for, because it was supposedly used by Williams during his miraculous 1941 season (he hit .406 that year, the last player to eclipse .400).

When he saw the bat, Williams closed his eyes and squeezed the handle.

"Yeah," he finally said. "This is one of my bats."

Someone asked how he knew.

> Take small steps. Don't let anything trip you up. All those steps are like pieces of a puzzle. They come together to form a picture. When it's complete, you've reached your ultimate goal, step by step. I can't see any other way of accomplishing anything.
>
> —Michael Jordan

"In 1940 and 1941," he said, "I cut a groove in the handle of my bats to rest my right index finger. I can still feel the groove."

Attention to detail doesn't get much more minute than that.

Companies succeed, and people succeed, because they don't allow for failure. FedEx tests its package sorters once each quarter for accuracy; anyone who doesn't score 100 percent is sent back for re-training. Sony tolerates only one failure among thousands of parts when evaluating the production of its camcorders. John Wooden used to show his incoming basketball recruits at UCLA how to lace up their shoes and put on their socks properly to avoid blisters.

Meanwhile, we live in a society that is much more tolerant of failure and imperfection: Over eighteen thousand pieces of mail will be mishandled

> *Don't be afraid to give your best to what, seemingly, are small jobs. Every time you conquer one, it makes you that much stronger.*
>
> —Dale Carnegie

in the next hour; fifty-five malfunctioning automated-teller machines will be installed and two hundred thousand incorrect drug prescriptions will be written over the next twelve months; and over one hundred incorrect medical procedures will be performed by the end of the day.

# Creativity
# (or, the Way We Imagine)

*The only factory asset we have is human imagination.*

—Bill Gates

I arrived in Orlando in June 1986 to promote a team that didn't exist. We were just trying to convince the NBA to even consider us as a potential franchise site. We had no arena, no community interest and no encouragement from the NBA. I spoke at service clubs, at business meetings, at conventions and churches. I spoke to whoever would have me. I developed a routine. I said, "Folks, when we get our team and it runs out onto the floor of the new arena, you'd better have your tickets. When Bird and Magic and Jordan come to town, you don't want to be on the outside, nose pressed against the glass, flapping your arms and yelling at me to open the doors. Because all I'll be able to tell you is that you should have ordered your tickets back then."

> *Imagination is the beginning of creation. We imagine what we desire. We will what we imagine, and at last, we create what we will.*
> —George Bernard Shaw
> WRITER

I think of that now on the nights our arena is sold-out, the aisles filled, the building warm with support. I think of that and I think of the story of one of my adopted sons, Brian, who, when he was thirteen and immersed in a grueling swimming lesson, stopped halfway through his laps.

"You can do that work, Brian," his coach told him.

"You just have to push yourself."

"I know I can do the work," Brian said. "But my head just won't let me."

It is our responsibility to free our imaginations, to dream beyond any limitations. It is our responsibility to dream wildly, to dream without boundaries.

Nobody did that better than Walt Disney. He once said, "Disneyland will never be completed. It will continue to grow as long as there is imagination in the world."

And yet so many of us tread through a corporate culture that drowns creativity and imagination. Our colleges and universities and MBA programs and law schools produce like-thinking drones, their attitudes tailored to fit the whims of accounting firms and law offices. We don't encourage new ways of thinking; we expect the young to perpetuate the old ways. And those who

> *The most important thing I learned from big companies is that creativity gets stifled when everyone's got to think within the box.*
> —David Kelley
> EXECUTIVE

don't think within that box are ostracized, like my mentor, Bill Veeck, whose outrageous ideas alienated him from baseball's establishment.

Much of what Jordan did was unprecedented in the NBA—his signature moves, his wagging tongue, his shaved head; he generated his own unique style. If we expect the upcoming generations to continue producing such unique genius, we have to encourage it. We have to applaud new ways of thinking instead of muffling them.

# Control
# (or, the Way We
# Comprehend the Limits of
# Our Responsibilities)

*If you get yourself too engrossed in things over which you have no control, it will adversely affect the things over which you do have control.*

—John Wooden

When I was in Spartanburg, South Carolina, in the 1960s, running the Phillies' minor-league club, I was a mess. I worried about the weather and about our lousy record and about how that might affect our attendance and about how that might affect my upward mobility. I worried about everything; I worried until I nearly tore out my stomach lining.

My boss was a wise man. His name was R. E. Littlejohn. He had a way with advice. One day he told me, "Control those things that you can control. Let the rest go."

I still struggle with that. It's hard to accept that things sometimes happen without your input, that there's nothing you can do to change them. I did what I could in Spartanburg, and I do what I can now; sometimes it doesn't feel like it's enough. But it is an overwhelming task taking care of ourselves, of our own responsibilities, without delving into the problems of others.

My children are growing up. I can't even control *them* like I used to. All I can offer them now is my attitude, my approach, and a promise that even if they do get a tattoo, I will still love them.

# CHAPTER SIX

# THE CHAMPION OF THE WHOLE WORLD

**JORDAN ON INFLUENCE:**

I think everyone, when they're kids, tries to pretend they're someone else. I'd be playing basketball with my friends, or with my older brother, and I'd get the ball, and I'd say, "I'm David Thompson" or "I'm Walter Davis," because they were older people who were playing

basketball in North Carolina.
When you're a kid, you don't want to emulate someone. . . . You actually want to be that person. You don't think of it in terms of wanting to grow up and be the same kind of person he is. You just want to be him, that's all.

*Whether we want to admit it or not, we're all hero worshippers. We don't have cowboys anymore. We don't have war heroes to admire. So most of the heroes today are athletes.*

—Bobby Bowden
*Florida State football coach*

hen he was a rookie in the NBA, Michael Jordan bought himself a coat. It was a Russian raccoon coat, thick and gaudy and made from expensive fur. To complement it, Jordan wore a host of glimmering necklaces and a few chunky rings. It wasn't his style, really, but he was copying, trying to ingratiate himself. He dressed the way he saw others dressing. When he showed up at the NBA All-Star game that season, the players froze him out. They refused to pass him the ball. Behind Jordan's back, they were talking. To them, the coat exemplified Jordan's attitude; he was seen as showy and self-centered and focused on the flash of his game.

"Whoever I was trying to be that first year," Jordan said, "it wasn't me."

So he changed his clothes. And he changed his image. He began wearing suits, mostly conservative in color and cut, yet with an understated elegance. Every night of his career, Jordan wore a suit, amid the frigid and sloppy Chicago winters, amid the stifling warmth of early summer. His career escalated; people began to watch him more vigilantly. He wore a suit for the brief walk from the hotel lobby to the team bus, from the team bus to the locker room, because every moment became an opportunity—to dignify himself, to elevate his image in the eyes of the children who idolized him.

"The fifteen seconds it takes for him to go from the elevator to the bus is the only time in some fan's lives that they might see him," wrote *Chicago Tribune* columnist Bob Greene. "Jordan wants those fifteen seconds to be dignified, because he knows those will be the fifteen seconds that they saw Michael Jordan." Greene continued, "Mike plays every game as if it were his last because he knows that in the stands are some fans who will never see him play again, other than that night."

"The day after Michael had a big game in the finals, I was standing up and eating at Al's Italian Beef on Taylor Street in Chicago," said Bulls fan Steve Rodheim. "Standing next to me was a huge African-American policeman. We

> *The word* influence *is the best one-word definition of leadership. Leaders are people who influence others to think, feel or act in certain ways.*
> —Hans Finzel
> AUTHOR

started talking about Michael and his performance. We talked about what Michael meant to the city of Chicago. I looked over and the policeman was sobbing. Big tears just rolling down his cheeks."

There is a story that writer Pete Hamill tells, set in the dusty hills of central Mexico. There, Hamill found a young boy herding goats, wearing a pair of tattered jeans, sneakers

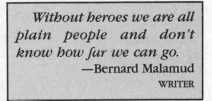

*Without heroes we are all plain people and don't know how far we can go.*
—Bernard Malamud
WRITER

tied with twine, and a bright red T-shirt with Jordan's No. 23 on the back. Hamill approached the boy and asked him how he'd become such a Michael Jordan fan here, thousands of miles from Jordan's direct sphere of influence.

*"Porque su papa fue aesinado,"* he whispered. *"Y todavia es el campeon de todo el mundo."*

Translation: "Because his father was murdered. And he is still the champion of the whole world."

In compiling anecdotes for this book, I spoke to a fan named Jack Cory, who was at an archaeological dig in Israel, just north of Jerusalem, when he came across a pair of young men who had been digging for seven years.

"Where are you from?" one of the men asked.

"Chicago," Cory said.

And one of the men replied: "Oh! Michael Jordan!"

In 1991, the Bulls were in Los Angeles to play the Lakers in the Finals. On the bus, the players were teasing each other about who knew the most famous people. The debate raged on and Michael remained quiet. Someone yelled, "How about you, Michael? Who do you know who's famous?" MJ said, "Who do you want me to call?" Someone said, "How about Janet Jackson?" MJ placed a call and said, "Hi, Janet. This is Mike. Give me a call." Someone said, "Aw, you're just faking it." Thirty seconds later, the phone rang. It was Janet Jackson. John Salley said, "That's when we knew there was us, and there was Michael Jordan!"

Tony Kornheiser, Washington sports writer, said, "I have a photo in my den that is very special. It was taken in a box on the night Jordan joined the Wizards. On the left is Ted Leonsis, then MJ, Abe Pollin and Bill Clinton. Let me tell you, Michael is clearly the focal point of the picture. You can *tell* that he is the sheriff."

## Top-Selling Issues of the *Chicago Tribune* since 1986:

1. Bulls Win 6th NBA Title
2. Bulls Win 3rd NBA Title
3. Bears Win Super Bowl XX
4. Bulls Win 4th NBA Title
5. Bulls Win 1st NBA Title
6. U.S. Fighters Attack Iraq
7. Bulls Win 2nd NBA Title
8. Bulls Win 5th NBA Title

Jordan is the anomaly, of course. Most of us are not afforded such great channels to influence people. We have to accomplish it on a smaller scale, amid our circle of acquaintances and family members and employees. But still, it is a crucial measure of our success as leaders: the attitude we leave in our wake. The example we set.

# The Presence of Greatness

*Few things are harder to put up with, than the annoyance of a good example.*

—Mark Twain

Jordan's influence on sport was as vast as any athlete's in the twentieth century. It is difficult to even quantify Jordan's effect upon the NBA itself. But the stories are universally glowing.

Vinny Del Negro was playing for San Antonio shortly after Jordan came back from baseball. He was guarding Jordan when they both went after a loose ball, and Del Negro grabbed Jordan by the arm, holding him back, and the ball tumbled out of bounds.

Jordan grinned. "You've learned a few things since I've been gone," he said.

"That stuck with me," Del Negro said. "The way he said it. The look in his eyes."

> At UCLA we have adopted twenty-three principles to guide our team. Why twenty-three? That's in honor of Michael's uniform number.
>
> —Steve Lavin
> UCLA BASKETBALL COACH

Jerome Williams, the Detroit Pistons forward, saw Jordan in the locker-room hallway after the Bulls had beaten Indiana in 1997 to make the NBA Finals. Williams was standing around, waiting for his ride, and Jordan walked past and greeted him and said, "I just wanted to tell you that you had a good year. You're a hard worker. You're going to make it."

"I'll never forget that," Williams said. "On MJ's big day, he encouraged me."

He did the same for so many of his teammates. With encouragement, with influence, he elevated their game. He empowered them. Jud Buechler, an unspectacular but steady member of the Bulls' championship teams, still remembers the first practice after Jordan came back from retirement. Jordan threw a pass, Buechler hit a shot, and Jordan gave him a high-five. *A high-five from Michael Jordan,* Buechler thought.

"I thought I was larger than life," Buechler said. "I

was ready to dive for loose balls, run through a wall. One little compliment from a guy like that is huge. If you're Michael Jordan and you come to practice and start giving guys compliments, it goes a long way."

"Late in my career, I was with the Cavs and we were playing the Bulls," said former NBA player Scott Brooks. "I'm standing at the top of the circle during a free throw, right next to Michael Jordan. I thought, *This is kind of cool.* Michael says, 'What's up, Scotty?' I thought, *He knows my name.* Then he says, 'Scotty, you've had a great career. You should be proud of what you've accomplished.' We were down by thirty at the time, but still—that made me feel so good."

We are all afforded this position at some point: with our children, with our employees, with those who respect our accomplishments. It is up to us to empower those who will eventually inherit our tasks, just as it is up to us to accept the advice of those who came before us.

"If I had been born on an island, learned the game all by myself and developed into the player I became without ever seeing another example, then maybe I would accept being called the greatest," Jordan said. "But I have used all the great players who came before me to improve upon my game. And somewhere, there is a little kid working to enhance what we've done. Unless they change the height of the basket or otherwise alter the dimensions of the game, there will be a player much greater than me."

Just as Jordan emulated Walter Davis and David Thompson before him, so do Grant Hill and Kobe Bryant and the hundreds of other journeyman pros in the league attempt—if even for a moment—to approach Jordan's genius. Even just to play against him was a thrill for the NBA's next generation; there was always that romantic hope that they might absorb the tiniest sliver of his magic.

"I always dreamed of playing against Michael Jordan," said forward Ben Wallace.

"When I first came into the NBA," said ex-pro Tom Tolbert, "I found myself watching MJ in amazement. That's not what you should be doing, but I felt like a fan."

When Don Reid was a rookie in Detroit, his coaches specifically warned him not to stare at Jordan. "I still did it," he said.

"I've saved every tape of every game I've played against Michael," said NBA veteran Dana Barros. "I'm saving them to show my kids."

Jordan's legacy in the athletic world is so immense that it transcends the boundaries of his sport, or even his gender; the fact is, by serving as an example, he subtly changed the attitude of many modern athletes.

The list of those who cite Jordan as a role model is virtually endless.

"I don't even know if he knows this or cares, but I have tried to emulate him on and off the field," said Derek Jeter, the New York Yankees short-stop, who first met Jordan when they played together in the Arizona Fall Baseball League. "He carries himself in a classy, dignified manner, and I think a lot of athletes could learn from his examples as a player and entrepreneur."

> *When you are in the presence of greatness, drop your pail in their well! You may never get a second opportunity. Greatness surrounds you like winds, every day. Your responsibility is to harness it, pull it toward you, and absorb it.*
> — Mike Murdock
> AUTHOR

One night, my son Alan, then eleven, was watching the Bulls play the Magic. He leaned over to my wife and said, "Michael doesn't have any tattoos, does he? I like that."

"Maybe we shouldn't have worked so hard to present a positive image," Jordan said. "But our thinking was always that people wanted to see a positive role model, someone who gets along with everyone."

"I want to have a positive impact on the players of today and the future," Jordan said, "but I worry some about money dominating the sport. I guess you can say that I'm part of it, but I have never let money affect the way I approached the game. It was far more important for me to know that I was going to be remembered for the way I played the game and not the commercials I made."

A chapter in author Roland Lazenby's book about the Bulls, *Blood on the Horns,* detailed Jordan's tough persona with his teammates; the New York Knicks gave a copy of the book to all of their players, hoping it would rub off. "MJ was Bobby Knight in short pants," Lazenby said.

It leads us back to Jordan's tireless practice habits, to his relentless work ethic—another of his legacies to the league's next generation. There was a time in 1993, Lazenby says, when the Bulls hit a lull in the schedule. They were tired of practice, tired of training, tired of each other. Coach Phil Jackson called for a practice, and the players sat in the training room and complained. Finally, Jordan said, "Let's go, millionaires," and on to practice they went. "He knew that, as a pro, that was your obligation," Lazenby said.

"I was a freshman at North Carolina, and we heard Michael was coming to practice," said NBA player Antawn Jamison. "Coach Smith let us play practice games that day. Everyone acted like it was a real game. MJ made everyone play at a higher level. Everyone elvated their game because no one wanted to disappoint him."

"When your best player puts it on the line every day, the other guys can't cut corners," said longtime NBA coach George Karl. "It's leading by example.

> *In 1996, after the Bulls swept the Magic in the play-offs, Michael told me, "Hang in there and don't get down. Your time is coming."*
> *I never forgot that.*
> —Shaquille O'Neal

They have to work at the same level as the top guy. That's what Michael did in Chicago and that's why the Bulls were so successful."

In April 2001, my wife Ruth and I flew to Boston for the Boston Marathon. Just prior to the flight, I began to experience flu-like symptoms. As hours passed and the race drew near, I was faced with the decision: Should I immediately return to Orlando, or should I "tough it out" and stay committed to the race?

It was more than my resolute, competitive nature that carried me to Hopkinton to participate in the race. During six of the most grueling, arduous hours of my life, it was the indelible image of Michael Jordan in the unforgettable "sick game" in the '97 finals against Utah that inspired me to finish the race. My mantra: "If Michael can play sick, then I can, too!"

What mattered more than money to Michael was respect. And reputation. The first time the Bulls' long-time broadcaster, Johnny "Red" Kerr, noticed this was in 1990, when Jordan refused to relent during a meaningless game against New Jersey. When it was over, Jordan told Kerr's wife that every game mattered, and that no matter the size of the crowd, he was striving to play that unattainable "perfect game." He figured he owed at least that much to the fans who adored him.

# The Power of Michael

This was in 1992, in Barcelona, the NBA's Dream Team on the cusp of the Olympics. Michael Jordan, Julius Erving, NBA coach Chuck Daly and television announcer Jim Gray were afforded the opportunity to play golf at a special course in the Pyrenees Mountains of Spain. Jordan, of course, has a strong affinity for golf. The only entry to this course was by helicopter, so the foursome left the hotel at 7:30 A.M., flew for an hour and a half, and set down at this golf club nestled in the mountains. There was no sign of people as they teed off, barely even a sign of civilization, except for a couple of club members. By the third hole, however, a small crowd began to gather; by the sixth hole, there were thirty people. By the ninth hole, there were a hundred people, and more straggling in from the surrounding mountains. By the fifteenth hole, the entire course was mobbed, people watching from fairways and greens, trampling all over the course. By the eighteenth hole, the crowd was five and six deep, nearly fifteen hundred people fighting for a glimpse. By the time the helicopter took off to bring them back to Barcelona, the crowd was swarming, people grabbing hold, desperate for a second's view.

"How did this happen?" Jim Gray said. "That's the power of Michael."

"To many, Michael Jordan is the prototype of a hero ... the Sir Galahad riding to the rescue ... and it has elevated him to such high proportions," wrote the *Chicago Tribune's* Sam Smith. "He's a Prince Charming, a storybook character, one of those things people carry in their hearts and their hopes."

Certainly, no athlete of his time has aroused as much passion from his fans as Jordan. Just ask the lady in Denver who lay down underneath the team bus and refused to leave until Jordan signed an autograph. Or ask Jordan himself, who has seen people nearly faint at the sight of him. They are rendered helpless and speechless, minds frozen in terror and wonderment, unable to convey a single coherent thought.

"People just seem to talk a little faster when they

talk to me," Jordan said. "They'll stutter a little bit and they'll be hurrying up what they say, like they have to say it very quickly, without pausing. I just try to listen the best I can. I don't consider it any kind of power on my part. I really don't. It's them assuming something about me."

My wife named a cat after Michael.
—Drew Goodman
DENVER NUGGETS' BROADCASTER

And the way Jordan combated this fear was by being unassuming, by ingratiating himself to people even in the briefest of interchanges. He'd combat their nervousness by displaying a coolness of his own, something that touched hundreds of fans who were afforded the unique opportunity of meeting Jordan. Like Bill Holmes, whose son, on his first day as a ball boy for the Bulls, missed the train to Chicago Stadium. When he arrived, Jordan considered him, coolly. "Who are you?" he said.

"I'm a new ball boy."

Jordan wrapped him in a playful headlock. "You're fresh meat," he joked. "But you're at home here."

He had an easy way with people, a power to connect with them. Sportswriter Jon Saraceno took his son to meet Jordan at a *Sports Illustrated* dinner. Jordan signed Sebastian Saraceno's book, then asked him, "Are you going to be in school tomorrow?"

When Jordan left, Jon Saraceno looked down at his son and saw he was crying.

"You all right?" he asked.

"I just met Michael Jordan," Sebastian said.

Jean Morse took her ten-year-old son to an IMAX theatre showing of Jordan's movie, and the lights went down, and in walked Jordan. The crowd exploded, and amid the din, Jordan picked out Jean Morse's son, bent down, looked him in the eye and asked, "Do you have all your homework done?"

"My son was awed," Morse said.

So was mine. His name is Richie, and one spring

> When I was at Tennessee, we visited Michael at his office in Chicago. He made us feel right at home the whole time.
> —Chamique Holdsclaw
> WASHINGTON MYSTICS

he was a ball boy for a Bulls-Magic game, and I introduced him to Michael Jordan. As Richie stood in frozen reverence, Jordan passed on this advice:

1. "If you want to do something and you love doing it, then do it."

2. "Whatever you choose to do, work hard at it."

3. "You've got to get it done in the classroom to be successful."

I think those mantras have been burned in Richie's psyche ever since.

This was something Jordan did often, making an extra effort with children. He never let it overwhelm him. He understood his impact was phenomenal. He'd ask the autograph-seeking kids who would hang outside the arena door during morning practices, "Why aren't you in school today?" When a road game forced him out of town on Halloween in his first year as a pro, he left a note for the children who knocked on his door: "Kids, sorry I missed you. If you still want to trick-or-treat, come back in three days." When two young boys knocked on his front door, asking Jordan's wife if he could come out and play, Jordan had just pulled into the driveway on his way home from the golf course. He got out and handed each of them a golf ball.

At his summer basketball camps, the kids often surveyed him with paralyzing awe. "But he makes people forget he's Michael Jordan, and makes them feel like they're the important person," said Donna Biemiller, who's worked at Jordan's camps. "At camp, they're so scared, but he allows the kids to relax with his sense of humor, and they have a memorable moment with him."

"I see people getting so nervous to meet me, and I know that I'm just some person, so why should I be nervous?" Jordan said. "If they're nervous meeting me, and I know that they have no reason to be, I have no reason to be nervous meeting anyone."

Michael runs a summer fantasy camp in Las Vegas for executives who pay twenty-five thousand dollars to play with MJ and other celebrities. Jordan is totally hands-on from 7:30 A.M. one-on-one games to late-night card games. Everyone stands in line to get a photo with Michael, including the coaches, some of the biggest names in the business.

These were not obligatory efforts, either. It mattered to Jordan to make a difference. On numerous occasions Jordan met with dying children before an All-Star game or a play-off game. Often, sessions that were supposed to last ten minutes went on for half an hour or longer. Jordan would sign autographs, pose for photos, learn names and include them in the conversation. Sometimes he came away with tear-stained eyes.

> *Early in life, I decided that I would not be overcome by events. Life is not easy for any of us, but it is a continual challenge, and it is up to us to be cheerful and to be strong, so that those who depend on us may draw strength from our example.*
>
> —Rose Kennedy

In the mid-1980s, Jordan attended a Nike summer retreat in Southern California. The final night a banquet was held, a rather prim affair with a Roaring Twenties theme, people dressed up, tables decorated. There were, as part of the decorations, filled water pistols in the centerpiece of each table. Before dinner was even served, former Stetson University basketball coach Murray Arnold, sitting a couple of tables away from Jordan, felt a spray of water on the back of his neck. He ignored it. Then came another. When he turned around, Jordan was giggling. Then Jordan started shooting at others, including the late Jim Valvano, and within five minutes, the place had become a battleground. It went on for forty-five minutes. Dinner was never even served.

"It all started with Michael Jordan," Arnold said. "Nobody else could get away with this. Michael's charisma was such that it went over. Michael gave them all a night they'd never forget."

# Like Father . . .

*There are not many Michael Jordans out there. Every kid wants to be, but they're not going to be. That's unrealistic. They have a better chance of being what their mother or father are; that's reality.*

—Charles Barkley

And yet for all of Jordan's universal impact, what mattered most was in front of him. His deepest influences were not Walter Davis or David Thompson or any of the other basketball stars of North Carolina. His deepest influences were his parents and his college coach, Dean Smith.

"He had taken from Carolina ... a sense of right and wrong and how you were supposed to behave on a basketball court and away from it, as well," wrote David Halberstam in his Jordan biography, *Playing for Keeps*. "He continued to clear many important decisions with his former coach, and certainly Dean Smith remained a living presence with him."

Jordan's greatest fear is of undoing his impact, of making a colossal mistake that would call into question all the positive energy he's generated. He's stumbled in the past, made small errors in judgment that have drawn sharp criticism, but he's never failed greatly enough to unravel his own image. And the reason it matters to him to maintain such a carefully drawn public persona centers on the people in his immediate vicinity: his wife, his children, his mother and his late father. In the end, this is the influence that truly matters.

> *Children have never been very good at listening to their elders, but they have never failed to imitate them.*
>
> —James Baldwin
> AUTHOR

"I know people are concerned about the behavior

> *After the games in Chicago, the media came at Michael in waves. The first wave came, then the second, then the third, then the fourth. At the back of the pack one day was a sixteen-year-old kid from the New Trier High School paper. Michael took as much time with him as he had with the major media. He did that kind of thing all the time. No matter how dumb the question, Michael would answer it like it was a great question.*
> —Chuck Swirsky
> BROADCASTER

of some young players, but it starts at home," Jordan said. "I've always said that. I wish some of the other guys in the league could have had fathers at home just to see what it's like; just to see how much better people they could be. . . . I want to have some influence on all my kids, but it's hard. My heroes were my parents. I can't see having anyone else as my heroes. When I talk to my kids sometimes, I can hear my own dad; the lessons he taught me. A smile comes to my face because you know what? I sound like him."

Not long ago, I got a note from Steve Schanwald, an executive vice president with the Bulls. He sent me a copy of a letter that I had sent him when I was the Philadelphia 76ers' general manager back in 1977, a brief word of encouragement to a young guy who was trying to break into the sports business. "I was cleaning out the attic the other day," he said, "and I came across this letter. I don't think there's anything more rewarding in our profession than helping young people climb the ladder of success. You were big-time back then and I wasn't, but you treated me like I was. Thanks for that."

Tony Kornheiser, the talented Washington sports columnist, observed: "MJ had such a dignity to his spirit, and he understood the responsibility of being a superstar. As a reporter in a major MJ press gathering, if you asked him a question and he used your first name in answering you—well, all your peers looked at you as if you were at an elevated plateu and had been bathed in celestial oil. It was like, Michael Jordan knows who I am!"

This is part of a letter that my daughter Karyn, as a freshman at Indiana University, wrote me three years ago. I share it with you as proof that influence, no matter how small or great, is always recognized.

> Dad, I've realized a lot of things since I've been away. I've realized that I have lived one of the most exciting, interesting lives and have had thousands of opportunities that could have only come to me through you. I am only now realizing how valuable they are. . . . I have notes that you've sent me hanging up in my room, and I don't think you realize how much they mean to me.

Perhaps she's right. Perhaps it's impossible for me to step away, to gain some dispassionate distance and fathom how much my words really meant to my daughter. But what matters to me, more than anything, is that Karyn knows.

# CHAPTER SEVEN

# THE KILLER IN CONTROL

JORDAN ON COMPETING AND WINNING:

The higher the stakes, the higher the rewards, the higher the level you play at. I've always had that. I think that's the mental part of the challenge. I love to hear them say they doubt me. That's something that's always driven me. You tell me I can't do something, and that's what I'm going to try to do.

*Former Coca-Cola Chairman Roberto Goizueta said that organizations that don't have an enemy need to create one. When asked why, he explained, "That's the only way you can have a war." In public, Coca-Cola may want to teach the world to sing, but their motto is "Destroy Pepsi."*

—Dr. Warren Bennis
*author*

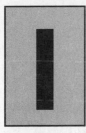t may sound like a bold statement, but there are volumes of evidence to prove that Michael Jordan is, quite simply, the greatest competitor this generation has ever seen. There is an interminable game being played inside his head; he will do whatever is necessary to win. He thrives on retribution. Every slight during his career was a major affront, every strong performance against him a jab in the eye.

I have heard dozens of corroborating stories in the midst of researching this book, so many that I cannot recount them all here without this chapter alone approaching the length of a Russian novel; but for the moment, let us explore the sad story of LaBradford Smith, whose name will be forever linked with the fury of Michael Jordan.

Smith was a marginal pro with the Washington Bullets who, one night in 1993, mustered thirty-seven points against the Bulls in Chicago. Then, afterward, according to Jordan, he muttered a facetious, "Good game." Jordan was furious. He said nothing on the plane ride to Washington, where the Bulls had to play another game against the Bullets. He ate nothing. He drank nothing. B. J. Armstrong walked back to speak to him. "Don't take this personally," Jordan said, "but tomorrow I've got to do what I've got to do."

Jordan nearly matched Smith's previous game total in the first half. He rode Smith defensively for the entire game. A few days later, the *Washington Post*'s David Aldridge looked into what had happened.

And what had happened is that Smith never said anything. Not one taunt. Not one word.

"Michael Jordan invented the story," Aldridge said, "to ignite a fury. To kill Smith and the Bullets."

"Michael was so competitive, it was almost abnormal," said former Bulls assistant coach Tex Winters. "He'd rip into his teammates, and I've often wondered why. I think it was his way of challenging himself. I think he was so much better than everyone that he had to do these things just to stay interested."

"I've never seen anyone like Michael Jordan who would fight so hard not to lose," said Washington Wizards owner Abe Pollin. "I've never seen anything like his drive."

MJ's comical, but intimidating repartee with

opponents not only reveals his supreme confidence, but also serves to embellish his legend. In Babe Ruth fashion, he called his shots:

**Vern Maxwell, NBA guard:** "In my third season we played Chicago. Before the tipoff, MJ came over and whispered, 'Max, I want you to string your shoes as tight as you can, because this is going to be a rough night for you.' In the second quarter he looked at me and said, 'Vern, did you string your shoes up like I told you?'"

**Tariq Abdul-Wahad, French-born NBA player:** "I was on the bench and MJ looked at me and said, 'Send the French guy out here.'"

**Mel Turpin, former NBA player:** "Michael dunked over one of our little point guards, prompting a fan to yell, 'Why don't you do that to someone your own size?' A few plays later, Michael dunked over my seven-foot frame, turned to the fan and said, 'Is he big enough for you?'"

**Butch Beard, former NBA coach:** "In the fourth quarter, I went to the scorer's table to check on a malfunctioning clock. MJ was kneeling, waiting to reenter the game and said, 'Coach, you don't need to be concerned about the clock. I'm going back in now, and I'm going to take over the game.' He did, too. He scored sixteen points in six minutes and the game was over."

**Chauncey Billups, NBA player:** "Right after I was drafted, Reebok did a commercial built around my quickness. The tag line was, 'He plays out of his shoes.' MJ saw me before opening night in Boston and said, "Welcome to the NBA, Rookie. And by the way, you better have your shoes on tonight because I'm going to run circles around you.'"

**Marques Johnson, former NBA player:** "At the 1986 NBA All-Star weekend in Dallas, I ended up in a limo with Patrick Ewing and MJ. Patrick said, 'I respect you, but don't be bringing your stuff into my office.' MJ replied, 'I've got a hide-and-seek show you haven't seen yet.'"

**Doug Collins, NBA coach:** "It was late in the game of my first night as the Bulls' coach, and we were in a dog fight at New York. Michael saw how intense I was and said, 'Get a drink of water. I'm not going to let you lose your first game.' He didn't either."

I witnessed Michael's competitive fire at the Bay Hill (Orlando) tournament. Arnold Palmer, Pennsylvania Governor Tom Ridge, Amy Grant and MJ were in the same foursome. Amy won the first hole and the crowd loved it. Michael came off the green wearing a scowl, barking, 'We got us a game going?'"

When Rex Chapman scored forty on him, Jordan responded in their next meeting with fifty. When Jerry Stackhouse scored nineteen points in the first half, Jordan held him scoreless in the second half—and scored forty-five points. "MJ might have a bad game," said veteran pro Sam Cassell, "but never bad back-to-back games."

When the Bulls trailed Vancouver by sixteen in the fourth quarter, Jordan scored eighteen consecutive points to win the game (afterward, the entire Bulls team ran up the tunnel and toward the locker singing the words to the Gatorade jingle, ". . . Like Mike! If we could be like Mike! . . .") When Matt Guokas was coaching in Orlando in 1991, he chose to double-team Jordan, and Horace Grant and Scottie Pippen carved up the Magic. Eight days later, the Magic traveled to Chicago, and Guokas refused to double-team Jordan. He scored sixty-four points, and he glided past Guokas the entire game with a sour look on his face, as if disappointed he wasn't being double-teamed (by the way, our Magic team won that game).

When Nikki McCray of the Washington Mystics kidded Michael that he should fear Kobe and Iverson if he comes back, MJ replied, "No, they should fear me."

He has crumbled entire franchises, almost as if casting a hex. His game-winning shot against the

Cleveland Cavaliers in the 1991 play-offs sent the entire Cavs franchise into a tumble. "It's never been the same since," said former Cleveland general manager Wayne Embry.

"If MJ was having a quiet game, I'd leave him alone," said former NBA player Dennis Scott. "If you waved your arms to stir the crowd, MJ took it personally. You just play your game and don't say anything. Anyone who gets into it with MJ will get whipped."

> *You can't imagine the pressure that's lifted off your shoulders when you have MJ on your team. Every time you walk on the floor, you're confident you have a good chance to win.*
> —Dennis Rodman

"You never wanted to do anything to get Michael Jordan riled up," said former Utah guard Jeff Hornacek.

Those who did say things saw Jordan's vengeful side. It could be wondrous to observe. He shot free throws with his eyes closed. He dunked on seven-foot centers. When John Long refused to shake his hand before a game, Jordan scored sixty-three. When George Karl criticized Jordan late in his career for being nothing more than a jump-shooter, Jordan scored forty-five—thirty-five of them on jump shots. When 76ers assistant Fred Carter kept yelling during a play-off game, "Make Michael shoot jumpers," Michael hit six in a row and hollered, "How's that,

Freddy?" When a Seattle writer mentioned that the Supersonics' Nate McMillan was out to stop him, Jordan spent an hour before the game watching tapes of McMillan. He scored forty that night; McMillan didn't score a point. In 1999, he emerged from retirement for an afternoon to school Bulls rookie Corey Benjamin in a game of one-on-one.

He'd telegraph his moves to defenders, tell them he would fake right this time, move left the next time, would shoot a jump shot here, and still they couldn't stop him. He vanquished egos.

One night while playing against Miami, Jordan began jawing at the Heat's well-coiffed coach, Pat Riley. Next possession, Jordan backed down his man in front of the Heat bench and asked Riley, "What do you want me to do, take a jump shot or drive?" Riley didn't answer. Jordan said, "Okay, I'll drive." And he threaded into the lane and dunked.

> *The American ideal is to win, unless you're playing against your grandmother. But even then you should try to win—unless you're mentioned in the will.*
> —Al McGuire
> COACH, BROADCASTER

Next time downcourt, Jordan asked the same thing. Riley didn't answer. "Okay," Jordan said. "Jump shot."

All net, of course.

"One day Michael and I were arguing about

something," said Washington Capitals owner Ted Leonsis, Jordan's business partner. "Suddenly he held six fingers up in the air. I asked, 'What's that mean?' He said, 'That's for six rings, so shut up. I know what I'm talking about.'"

My son Brian swam in the Junior Olympics when he was fifteen. He was talented, and I always thought he could have had a great deal more success than he did. So one night I asked him why he didn't.

"Doesn't it get your blood pumping standing up on those blocks?" I asked. "When you're getting ready to swim?"

"Dad," he said, "I really appreciate your motivational speeches. They're very good. But honestly, it doesn't."

"But what about the competition?" I said.

"Dad," he said, "the competition doesn't mean that much to me. I'm going to chill out. I don't plan on doing that much competing."

Perhaps this is merely proof that my son doesn't like swimming, or doesn't like working, or doesn't *really* like my motivational speaking. But I prefer to think of Brian as the exception to the rule. I like to think that he will come around eventually, because he will have to come around. Because as much as we like to push ourselves (and rightfully so) to be caring and compassionate, in the end, we must compete to win, and we must win in order to succeed.

"Competition has shaped every facet of our society," said author and speaker Harvey Mackay. "It is the essence of motivation. It's the reason we set annual sales goals and post monthly standings. It's the reason we get results. Competition is what drives performance in every field. Let's stop treating competition as if it were wrong. It's not. It's our strongest motivator for improving ourselves and the world in which we live."

One of the corporate values at ServiceMaster Corporation is, "There are no friendly competitors."

St. Louis Cardinals manager Tony La Russa said, "You don't manage for the money or the publicity. It's about the competition."

> *Michael played hard, but all players play hard. The difference was he outcompeted people. That's a rare trait. You can't just play hard, you have to compete hard. There is a great difference.*
>
> —Kelvin Sampson
> COLLEGE BASKETBALL COACH

"Every time I step on the court, if you're against me, you're trying to take something from me," Jordan said. "I don't want the other team to win. I just do not want them to win."

"I was with Minnesota, and we were beating the Bulls

at home," said former NBA guard Pooh Richardson. "Tony Campbell was guarding Michael, and said to him, 'This is it. We're going to beat you guys.' Michael said, 'You wouldn't beat me if your life depended on it.' Then Campbell hit a shot to put us up by one with five seconds to go. Michael took the ball, whirled into the lane, made an underhand scoop shot, and the Bulls won the game. I've never seen anything like it."

After he lost eight straight games of Ping-Pong (for twenty-five dollars each) to Chicago sportswriter Lacy Banks, Jordan reportedly bought a table for his house and hired a coach to work with him. A few weeks later, Jordan won seven of eight games against Banks, then never played him again.

When Jordan was a kid, he would wager household chores in games against his sisters. He wanted to win so badly that he could never resist a bet. He also wanted to win so badly that he didn't always hold to the

> Everytime I lose, I die a little.
>
> —George Allen
> FORMER NFL COACH

rules. He once paid off the porter at the airport to ensure his bag would come out first, and then bet his team-mates on it. When he lost a game of Go Fish to Buzz Peterson, his college teammate, and Peterson's mother, Jordan sulked. When he lost two dollars in a college poker game, he was furious. When he lost to former

North Carolina assistant coach Roy Williams at pool, he refused to speak to Williams the next day. When he was losing a pinball game to teammate Matt Doherty, he made Doherty stay up all night and play.

Once Jordan played pool against Doherty and lost. Afterward, Michael tossed his cue onto the table and declared, "This table is not regulation."

> *To be successful you have to like to lose a little less than everybody else.*
> —Phil Jackson

In college, after a grueling practice, he would insist on running races in the parking lot against his teammates. "Michael would deny this, but he never won a race," said UNC teammate Joe Wolf. "Buzz Peterson and Kenny Smith were faster and would always beat him. But afterward, Michael would always say, 'Let's go again.' He knew that to get faster, he had to run against faster people."

He had a wicked memory. He never forgot a loss. And he never forgot to collect on a bet. Once he sent a clubhouse boy to collect five dollars from NBA veteran Vin Baker, on a bet that Baker insists Jordan *lost*. "Sometimes," said ex-Bulls coach Phil Jackson, "he'd come to me and say, 'Coach, you know, you still owe me two dollars.' And it would be from some free throws he'd hit in practice months ago."

It wasn't about the money, of course. It was about the trophy. It was about confidence and bragging rights. It was about the last word. When someone would offer to bet him on something, and they'd ask how much, Jordan would often reply, "Whatever makes you nervous."

One night, soon after he made his return to the NBA from baseball, Jordan sat down in the fourth quarter with the Bulls leading Utah comfortably. He had forty-nine points. He turned to the crew on press row and asked, "What's the league high-scoring game this year?"

> *I love this game and I love competing. I love it when I get hit and when I hit back.*
>
> —Steve Young
> FORMER NFL QUARTERBACK

Somebody called back, "Karl Malone, fifty-four points."

Jordan checked back into the game, scored three quick baskets, and sat down again. "Now the high is fifty-five," he said.

This is a man whose assumed name when he checked into hotels was that of the teammate, Leroy Smith, who beat him out for the varsity basketball team in tenth grade. He remembered criticisms that out-of-town reporters had written years before, and he remembered challenges that had been issued months before. In an interview with ESPN's Dan Patrick immediately after the 1998 finals, Patrick joked about being able to take Jordan one-on-one, and Jordan challenged him right there.

"Just minutes before, this guy hit one of the biggest shots in basketball history," Patrick said. "Then he wants to play me just to shut me up."

He had a goal of dunking on every center in the league. He even dunked

> *Before the first game of a Bulls–Miami Heat play-off series, Michael went out to meet the refs. He shook Keith Askins's hand, but he ignored Alonzo Mourning. That was MJ's way of getting into Zo's head.*
> —Ike Austin
> NBA PLAYER

on his own teammate, Corie Blount, during a celebrity game. He spent a great deal of effort trying to dunk on the Hawks' rangy shot-blocker, Dikembe Mutombo, and when he finally did, in a play-off game after Jordan emerged from retirement, he taunted Mutombo with a waggle of his finger.

"I told you I'd dunk on you," Jordan told him. "That's why I came back."

"Michael would take any little thing someone said and create a challenge for himself to beat that person or team," said Lakers center Shaquille O'Neal. "He kept his edge because he just made up stuff in his mind. You did not want to make Michael mad."

Jordan's instincts led him astray at times. This was the side effect. With such a finely honed competitive instinct, it was nearly impossible to let go. Said Phil Jackson: "The greatness of Michael Jordan is his competitive drive. The weakness of Michael Jordan is his competitive drive."

When Jordan was embroiled in a controversy after taking a gambling trip to Atlantic City during an NBA play-off series against the Knicks, his own father admitted that what Jordan had was not a gambling problem, but a competition problem. "But if he didn't have a competition problem," James Jordan said, "nobody ever would have written about him in the first place, and he never would have gotten to the level he did."

What you may not remember is that, in the midst of the Atlantic City controversy, the Bulls won that series against the Knicks. "The media ripped Michael," said Knicks general manager Ernie Grunfeld, "but all that did was wake him up. He was saying, in effect, 'I'll always be there to do my job. And if you arouse me, I'll really destroy you.'"

That's the thing. Outside influences never affected his job. On a night during the 1992 NBA Finals in Portland, Jordan was sitting in his room with a few of his old friends from North Carolina, and they were riding him, talking trash about his game. This was around ten at night, and Jordan said, "All right, let's see you back it up."

> *I want to be the best. Maybe not the best coach, but the best winner. You can name me the worst coach if you give me twenty rings. I want to win.*
> —Doc Rivers
> COACH, ORLANDO MAGIC

They drove to a Nike facility and Michael opened up the gym and they played pickup games late into the night.

The next day against Portland, Jordan put up forty points.

A healthy measure of competition, kept in perspective, is crucial. It breeds confidence, which helps us to overcome obstacles, to take risks, to allay our fears and to win. Six NBA championship rings were not attained by backing away from a challenge.

# Building Wings

This was in Chicago, during a game between the Bulls and Hawks that came down to the final moments. There were twenty seconds left and Steve Kerr had the ball for Chicago and began to drive toward the basket, and as he did, Jordan, sensing Kerr's move wasn't going to work, called a time-out. After the time-out, the ball went to Jordan, isolated on Mookie Blaylock. He hit the shot. He won the game.

He always wanted the ball in these situations. He almost always got the ball. When he didn't, he was infuriated. During spring training in 1994, when

Jordan was playing baseball, he played in a pickup basketball game. He scored every basket, but on the last play, his manager, Terry Francona (against whom Jordan spent the entire season embroiled in an ongoing game of Yahtzee), missed a wide-open shot that would have won the game.

"Don't ever do that again," Jordan said. "In any game, I take the last shot."

He was supremely confident. He never considered that he could be denied the basketball, or that he could be denied his shot. In Game Three of the 1991 NBA Finals, when the Bulls faced the Lakers, the Los Angeles coaches

> *There's an elation to winning.*
> —Joe Paterno

specifically instructed their players not to allow Jordan to touch the ball on Chicago's last possession. "The play started," recalled Lakers assistant Bill Bertka, "and Michael got the ball, raced down the court and scored. The Bulls won and went on to sweep us. That was so typical of MJ."

So typical that a nearly identical scenario had occurred in 1989, with the Bulls leading the Knicks 3-2 in a play-off series. Late in the game, the Knicks led by one, and New York coach Rick Pitino called time-out. "Whatever we do," Pitino said, "we're not going to be beaten by Michael Jordan. Do not allow him to catch the ball. I want two of you to deny him, and if he does get it, double-team him immediately."

Jordan fought off the defenders. He got the ball. He dribbled through a trap, got fouled, hit both free throws, won the game and ended the series.

Once, in the fourth quarter of a game against Phoenix, Jordan stood next to former Suns coach Cotton Fitzsimmons on an inbounds play and declared, "Cotton, I want you to know it's all over now."

"My rookie year with the Clippers, we're up on the Bulls at home by five with forty seconds left," said the Memphis Grizzlies' Lorenzen Wright. "We had the ball out of bounds. We inbounded into the backcourt, which gave the Bulls the ball. Michael hit a three. Then Michael intercepted Rodney Rogers's pass and hit a shot at the buzzer to tie it. We went ino overtime and the Bulls won. What an introduction to Michael."

"My rookie year, we're in Chicago and up by one late in the game," said the Hawks' Chris Crawford. "MJ hit a bank shot to put the Bulls up by one. Then we came down and Steve Smith got fouled. He hit them both and we're back up by one. The last play of the game MJ hit a jumper and the Bulls won. MJ walked off the floor like

> *I think I'm lucky. I was born with very little talent, but great drive.*
> —Anthony Quinn
> ACTOR

it was no big deal—just another day at the office. He had forty-nine that night."

On what was supposed to be a day off for him before the 1996 play-offs, Jordan arrived at the gym wearing a pair of sweatpants and worn-out canvas sneakers. He wanted to join the team's scrimmage, but Phil Jackson had insisted that he sit out, take it easy. Jordan couldn't resist. He laced up his canvas sneakers and barged onto the court.

"Michael was all over the place, making steals and blocks," recalled his former teammate, John Salley. "One play he made a steal and dunked right over me. As he's soaring over me, he said, 'Try to block this one.' I thought to myself, now I understand."

> *While the law of competition may be hard sometimes for the individual, it is best for the race, because it ensures the survival of the fittest in every department.*
> —Andrew Carnegie

Former Bulls teammate, Charles Davis, understood as well. He said, "When I practiced against MJ I never backed down because he wouldn't allow you to. If you slacked off against him, he'd bury you because he felt you were cheating him. Michael knew the harder he was pushed in practice, the better he'd play in the games."

"Michael's rookie year in Chicago, we came out of

training camp one night and we're walking to my car," said former Bull Rod Higgins. "It was late and dark and we heard a dog bark.

"I said, 'Michael, do you hear that dog?'

"Michael said, 'Yeah.'

"Then the barking got louder and closer and out of nowhere we saw this big German shepherd running after us. We started running around the car. Michael left me in the dust. Even threw a couple of elbows at me. He wasn't going to let the dog or me beat him.

"Michael ended up jumping on the hood of my car. He left a dent in it. Finally, the dog left. I guess he had bigger fish to fry."

"Michael had a mean streak," said ex-Bulls coach Doug Collins. "He could be vicious. All the great geniuses of the world were like that. We're talking about the Einsteins, the Edisons, the Roosevelts. These people came across something and worked to perfect it. You played one-on-one with Michael, and he was not going to let you score."

We cheat ourselves when our self-esteem falters. Lack of confidence is the primary reason that we shy away from competition, and without competition, there is no possibility for success. But confidence can be built—if we are willing to face those things we fear, and if we are

> *Franklin Roosevelt was the only person I ever knew—anywhere—who was never afraid.*
> —Lyndon B. Johnson

willing to take the risks. For most of us it is not a matter of playing hurt, or taking the final shot, or fighting for victory in such an overt sense. It is more subtle, something that exists in the environments we cohabit, in the classroom or the boardroom or the sales floor. It is an urge to succeed that overwhelms our urge to take the easy way out.

Historian Jeffry D. Wert observed that trait in studying the life of Confederate General Robert E. Lee: "A Texan in the Confederate Army compared Lee's temperament to that of 'a game cock.' The mere presence of an enemy aroused his pugnacity," he wrote, "and was a challenge he found hard to

> *If we listened to our intellect, we'd never have a love affair. We'd never have a friendship. We'd never go into business because we'd be cynical. Well, that's nonsense. You've got to jump off cliffs all the time, and build your wings on the way down.*
> —Ray Bradbury
> AUTHOR

decline." General James Longstreet described this trait in Lee as "headlong combativeness." Lee's battle correspondence bristles with words like "destroy," "ruin," "crush," and "wipe out" when referring to what he wanted to do to Union armies.

"We had beaten the Bulls regularly through MJ's

first six seasons," said former Detroit Pistons general manager Jack McCloskey. "After we beat the Bulls in the 1990 play-offs in Detroit, I saw Michael outside the arena, leaning against a pole. I stopped and talked to him. He was really dejected. He said, 'Jack, are we ever going to beat you guys?' I told him to hang in there. The rest is history."

"I will die with no bullets in my holster," Jordan said. "Like with injuries, you have to ask yourself what they mean. How bad are they? One time I sprained my ankle, and my whole foot was huge. It happened in a game, and I retaped it, laced up my shoe and kept playing. We traveled home and I kept it in ice and elevated it, iced it the whole next day, and that night I scored sixty-four against Orlando. . . . It's all a mind game. Maybe some of it is genetic. I don't know if you can teach it, because it's internal. . . . I hope people who hear my stories can look inside themselves and maybe push a little harder."

> When I was in college, I found out that the MVPs and all-league team and all that are hugely political. So I decided that if I win every game, that becomes historical fact, not anyone's opinion.
>
> —Bill Russell

Early into his second year as a professional, Jordan broke his foot. The Bulls wanted him to sit out the season, many observers said, because they wanted to

> *His mind-set was at least part of what made him as successful as he was. He was completely uncompromising. This kind of mind-set, this obsession, fuels winning in sports. Grove couldn't accept the idea of losing.*
> —Jim Kaplan, AUTHOR ON HALL OF FAME PITCHER LEFTY GROVE

improve their status in the NBA draft lottery. Jordan refused. He couldn't accept the idea of purposeful defeat. Even though the Bulls were nearly twenty games under .500, he still thought he could lead them to the play-offs. And he did. And in a play-off series against the Celtics, Jordan had his first transcendent moment on the national stage, scoring sixty-three points in defeat.

He played to win. His urge was strong enough to deny sickness and pain, to turn them from debilitating factors into kindling for his fury. Once he left a play-off game against Atlanta on a stretcher and came back to score twenty in the fourth quarter for the win. Before the legendary Sick Game at Utah in the 1997 finals, Jordan's anger was directed toward the Bulls franchise, toward the team doctors who couldn't heal him fast enough, toward the choice of team hotel in the suburbs of Salt Lake City, which led Jordan to eat the lousy pizza he'd consumed the night before, and which, in Jordan's mind, had made him sick. "He used all this stuff to motivate himself," said Chicago sportswriter Rick Telander. "To play with an edge."

Sports columnist Mike Lupica once had a Jordan motivation experience: "In 1996, MJ was back from baseball and came to New York for a game. The Bulls practiced at the Reebok Club on the west side of Manhattan. Michael came out and headed to the bus when he saw me off to the side. We chatted and then he said, 'Last year on your television show, you said I'd lost a step. Do you still think I've lost a step?' I said, 'No, I don't.' He smiled like a ten-year-old and walked to the bus. I thought, 'There is nothing he won't do to motivate himself.'"

On Valentine's Day 1990, Jordan's uniform was stolen before a game at Orlando. "I'm not mad at you," Jordan told Magic trainer Keith Jones, "but you all will have to pay."

"And we did," Jones said.

When the Bulls played the Nets one night, with the Nets streaking and the Bulls in the midst of a lull, New Jersey Nets broadcaster Mike O'Koren declared to Jordan during a pregame interview that the Bulls would lose.

Jordan was tying his shoes. He looked up and said, "What?"

"The Nets are going to beat you tonight," O'Koren said.

"No," Jordan said. "That's not going to happen."

He had thirty-five points after three quarters. The
Bulls won easily. Late in the game, he hit a shot to seal
the victory and backpedaled downcourt and looked
over at O'Koren and
shook his head.

> *Our doubts are traitors,*
> *and make us lose the good*
> *we oft might win, by fear-*
> *ing to attempt.*
> —William Shakespeare

He wore a small pad on
one of his knees, and if his
knee hurt, he'd switch the
pad from one leg to the other so the other team
wouldn't know if he was injured. He would come back
and play the next day on sprained ankles, on sore feet,
on bad knees. "His pain threshold was remarkable—so
far beyond normal players," said former Bulls general
manager Rod Thorn. "He just wouldn't be left out. He
had to compete and beat you."

Former NBA player Kenny Smith remembered, "When
I played at North Carolina, all the NBA guys would come
back to play in the summer. During the scrimmages,
Michael would never leave the court. Not even for a
drink of water. Between games, he'd stand out at mid
court. I asked him why and he said, 'I don't need water. I
don't need anything. I'm not leaving the whole time.'"

When we learn to take chances, when we learn to
see past our fears, we reach a point of near-invincibil-
ity. Certainly, we cannot avoid losses, and we cannot
eliminate setbacks, but they will begin to slide off our

backs. And then anything is possible, because we believe it ourselves.

Wayne Gretzky's statement about Tiger Woods confirms that thought: "When I watch golf and hear other players interviewed, most of them sound like they can't believe they won. Then you hear from Tiger, and he either expected to win or he can't believe he didn't. It's a different mind-set altogether."

"I was with Minnesota and checked into the game to guard Michael," said NBA player James Robinson. "He said to Scottie Pippen, 'I've got a guinea pig on me.' Then he said to me, 'I'm going to score on you.' Next three plays, he posted me up and hit three straight hoops. I left the game and Michael patted me on the butt and said, 'I'll see you later.'"

"One night when I was an assistant with the Hawks, we were playing the Bulls in Atlanta," said NBA assistant coach Johnny Davis. "Dominique Wilkins made a sensational shot to give them the lead late in the game. No time-out for the Bulls. They cleared a side for Michael. He took the ball, turned his head toward our bench and winked at us. He faked baseline, turned back the other way and slammed it down over everybody.

"Then he ran past our bench and winked at us again."

# A Con Game

All of these stories make Jordan sound like a ruthless soldier, like a merciless man without the capacity for friendship or compassion. But the truth is a great deal less rigid than that. Jordan's effervescent personality, that subtle upturned smile—these were weapons as much as anything else. New York Knicks coach Jeff Van Gundy once called Jordan a "con man." Although Jordan was very angered by the accusation, it was meant to be a compliment. "He was so into winning, he'd befriend the other players and the refs and they didn't even know it," Van Gundy said. "He knew every button to push. The guys wanted to be liked by him so much they had a hard time competing against him."

"He had the competitive arrogance," said University of Connecticut coach Jim Calhoun, "but it didn't leave the court."

It wasn't that Jordan played nice on the court. In fact, he was one of the most prolific trash-talkers in NBA history. Even in pickup games, where Jordan was (and still is) known to resurrect his magic just because he can (one Chicago fan remembered Jordan singing his own Gatorade theme song—"Sometimes I dream, that he is me . . ."—after winning a pickup game); and even in his own fantasy camps, where Jordan once joined a team that trailed by twenty points with five minutes to play and led them into overtime.

One of his teammates in Chicago, Michael Holton, was guarding Jordan in practice shortly after he returned from his foot injury in 1986, and Jordan yelped, "Don't make me open that can!"

Holton didn't respond. Next day, Jordan said the same thing to him. Holton began to guard Jordan more closely, and Jordan got madder until finally he said, "All right, I'm opening the can."

"What's in the can?" Holton said.

"A butt-kicking," Jordan replied.

"That was the highlight of my time with the Bulls," Holton said. "I made Michael open the can."

During Erick Strickland's rookie season with Dallas, he saw Jordan in a restaurant. Strickland introduced his aunt to him. Jordan said, "Make sure to get him home right away, because it's going to be a long night for him tomorrow."

Once, against Boston, the Celtics were beating the Bulls in their home opener, and the Celtics were talking a little too much. They were lined up for a free throw and Jordan said, "I'm getting this rebound."

The free throw was missed. Jordan got the rebound. He scored and was fouled.

> *I was with Boston, playing at Chicago. I'm alone on Michael and he said, "Watch this." He started to back me down, and before he jumped, he shouted, "Aaaah!" Like I fouled him. And the ref called the foul.*
>
> —Ron Mercer
> NBA PLAYER

He could talk up a storm himself, but he couldn't stand others taunting him. Brian Shaw, then with Golden State, once had a good night against Jordan and started jabbering too much, and Jordan turned to Warriors coach P. J. Carlesimo and said, "Tell Brian Shaw to be quiet." Shaw kept talking. Jordan said to Carlesimo, "I'm warning you." And then he scored twelve straight points to win the game. And as he walked off the court, he said to Carlesimo, "I told you to leave me alone."

Ric Bucher of *ESPN* magazine has a vivid memory of Jordan the competitor: "In 1998 I went to a Bulls shoot-around and saw an amazing sight. Michael was going one-on-one with Scott Burrell at the highest level of intensity. MJ was down 9–7 but won 11–9 and was talking the whole time. As Burrell walked toward me I asked, 'What did you do to deserve that?' Jordan heard me and said, 'Talking.' I was stunned— here was Michael at the end of his career and got his hackles raised to the point he had to whip up on a journeyman player at a shoot-around!"

Former NBA player Sam Bowie observed, "MJ could

talk trash with you, but it was positive trash. It was almost complimentary, and not belittling or degrading. Mike would score on you and then pat you on the butt, and it made you feel you almost liked what he'd just done to you."

> *If being an egomaniac means I believe in what I do, then, in that respect, you can call me that. I believe in what I do, and I'll say it.*
> —John Lennon

The closest I came to talking trash with Michael Jordan was when I played in Charles Barkley's charity golf tournament in Orlando one summer. Our group was one foursome ahead of Jordan's group. We got backed up on a tough par three that looked down into a valley, and by the time I teed off, all of Jordan's followers had gathered around the tee to watch. I was petrified; I hadn't hit a decent shot all afternoon.

From behind me, Michael muttered, "Let's see what this guy can do."

I steadied myself and swung. Somehow, I managed to land my drive within five feet of the pin. As I walked off the tee, I heard Michael say, "You can tell that Pat doesn't spend much time at the office."

Jordan knew how to play the game within the game. The psychological war. He knew exactly how far to let it go. "MJ would never play dirty," said referee Hubert Evans. "But he'd always react when it

> *During my rookie season in Charlotte, I tied up a loose ball with Jordan. Then I won the jump ball. Greatest jump ball of my career. It's probably something I'll brag about to my kids someday.*
>
> —Malik Rose
> NBA PLAYER

started." When New York's Chris Childs threw a basketball at Jordan in a fit of misguided anger, Jordan flashed, for an instant, a burst of raw rage. And then he backed away.

"A killer in control," Pat Riley has called him.

"My grandparents used to always say, 'Think before you act, and always be in control at all times,'" Jordan said. "I always remember that."

And so he could attack when needed and he could make friends when needed. Either way, he'd maintain control. Either way, he'd win. And there was a part of him that cultivated friendships and encouraged opponents because he didn't want to discourage his opponents entirely; he relished the aftermath of a difficult victory. He once thanked his friend Buzz Peterson for being named North Carolina high school player of the year because it gave him a reason to outdo him in college. The reason that he retired the first time was because all of the challenges were gone. "I really think MJ wanted the other players to play up to his level," said veteran pro Hersey Hawkins. "It was more challenging to him to have other guys competing at his level."

Still, there were those who saw through Jordan's amiable nature. George Karl tried to counteract it in the 1996 NBA Finals. He told his Seattle Supersonics team that he didn't want to be friends with Michael, and that he didn't want them to be friends with Michael,

> *Cultivate a healthy respect for your competitors, but never overestimate or underestimate them. Never forget that, no matter how highly one or more of them may be regarded, if you make the mistake of holding them in awe, you will lack the will to beat them.*
>
> —Al Kaltman
> AUTHOR

either. He delivered a ten-minute speech, giving specific instructions to everyone from point guard Gary Payton to his son, a ball boy. Jordan never shook Karl's hand the entire series. Never even looked at him. "I thought I was the macho guy," Karl said, "but MJ outraged *me*."

"One night when Michael was sick, I scored twenty-four and he scored twenty-one," said former NBA player Craig Ehlo. "The next day, Sam Smith quoted me in the *Chicago Tribune:* 'If you're sick, you should stay home from school.' Our next game against the Bulls, Michael scored fifty-five on me. I should have kept my mouth shut."

There are three lessons to be taken from this. The first is that politeness can be a disarming strategy when competing. The second is that the politeness of others can be a disarming strategy when competing. And the third is that there is a time, in the midst of competition, to let politeness fade for the moment.

It was difficult not to place Jordan on some higher plane. Rarely, if ever, has sports been blessed with such a pure competitor, a man whose lone goal was victory by whatever means necessary. He was intimidating, he was fearless, he was driven and the legacy of his competitive nature is like none to come along in generations.

It continues to trickle down in the residue of memories like those of veteran pro Larry Robinson, who on the first night of his rookie season in Washington in 1991 was assigned to guard Jordan. Jordan had powdered resin on his hands, and as he touched fists with his opponents, bits of powder burst from his hand. The Bullets won the opening tap, and Jordan backpedaled to play defense. What Robinson didn't realize was that Jordan kept powder inside his fists as well. Michael raised his arms, opened his hands, and the powder sprinkled down upon him like fairy dust.

# CHAPTER EIGHT

# THE FIST

**JORDAN ON TEAMWORK:**

There are plenty of teams in every sport that have great players and will never win titles. Most times, these players aren't willing to sacrifice for the greater good of the team. The funny thing is, in the end, their unwillingness to sacrifice only makes individual goals more difficult to achieve.

*A great player can only do so much on his own, no matter how breathtaking his one-on-one moves. If he is out of sync psychologically with everyone else, the team will never achieve the harmony needed to win.*

—Phil Jackson

rant Hill held up one of his hands. He stretched five rangy fingers at me, spreading them as far apart as they would go.

"These," he said, "are the five members of a basketball team."

We were sitting in the locker room in Orlando. It was Hill's first year with the Magic after six years with the Detroit Pistons, but he was reaching back further, to his years at Duke, to a speech that his coach, Mike Krzyzewski, used to give.

Hill waggled his fingers. "These," he said, "do not become very effective until they are joined together tightly." He balled his hand into a fist. "This," he said, "can cause much more damage than five fingers sticking in different directions."

Hill relaxed his hand, so that the fist became a jagged creature with a couple of fingers splayed apart.

"If one or two stick out," he said, "that's not a very effective fist."

That, Hill said, became the rallying cry for a Duke team that won NCAA titles in 1991 and 1992. It is a vivid illustration of a principle that interlopes on the worlds of both sports and business: the notion of teamwork.

It was something that Michael Jordan did not accept when he entered the NBA. At first, he tried bullying his way to a championship. He had the idea that he could hoist an entire team on his shoulders and lead it through the play-offs. In retrospect, it's easy to understand why he felt this way. Those early teams Jordan played on in Chicago were not exactly blessed with grade-A talent. It was his show, and nobody else's. He had no one to rely on, no one to depend upon besides himself. But when Jordan scored sixty-three against the Celtics in the 1986 play-offs, his team still lost. And the Celtics, with Larry Bird, with Kevin McHale, with Robert Parish and Dennis Johnson and Danny Ainge, did not lose.

> In 1983, Michael was kind of full of himself and dogging it at practice. Dean Smith had a rule that if you dogged it, the whole team had to run extra. So Dean stopped practice, put a chair in the middle of the floor, and told Michael to sit and watch while the rest of the team ran. I think that was a defining moment for Michael.
>
> —David Chadwick
> PASTOR AND AUTHOR

By the end of his career, Jordan had developed a complex symbiosis with his teammates. Together they earned those six championship rings.

If there is one concept that I have studied more than others in my years as an NBA executive, it's that of teamwork. I have presided over terrible teams (we won't get into details) and champion-

> *You want your company to run well? Here's an iron-clad rule: Get everyone on the same team. Get every-one working for the same team. Get everyone working for the same goal; get them to win or lose together.*
> —Gordon Bethune
> CEO OF CONTINENTAL AIRLINES

ship teams (I won't brag, though I certainly could, if you ask) and I have isolated those elements that make up the difference. Call it chemistry or bonding or mutual acceptance or any of the above. The absolute truth is that sports franchises fail— just as corporations fail—

> *Without everybody em-bracing what we want to do, we haven't got a prayer.*
> —Jack Welch
> CEO OF GENERAL ELECTRIC

without teamwork.

No surprise, then, that teamwork has become one of those buzzwords for corporate America. A great many of my public-speaking clients ask me to address this topic, whether to a grand ballroom of *Fortune 500* CEOs or a banquet hall filled with small-business

> *Business—and this means not just the business of commerce, but the business of education, the business of government, the business of medicine, is a team activity. Always, it takes a team to win.*
> —Andrew Grove
> CEO OF INTEL

owners. They're all curious about the same thing: is what happens in sports transferable to the business world?

The obvious answer is: Yes. Of course. The less obvious question is: *How* is it transferable to the business world?

I spent a few years looking into this. I even wrote a book about it, *The Magic of Teamwork*. What I attempted to discern were the defining characteristics of great teams. What follows are my eight primary findings, dovetailed to the experience of Michael Jordan.

> *When you don't take care of the team first, the baseball gods won't let you get away with it.*
> —Todd Hundley
> MAJOR-LEAGUE CATCHER

## 1. Talent

*You can take an old mule and run him, feed him, train him and get him in the best shape of his life, but you ain't gonna win the Kentucky Derby.*

—PEPPER MARTIN
*former major-league baseball star*

I owe this one to Jack Ramsay, the longtime NBA coach and broadcaster, who looked at my list of great team characteristics and told me—as B. J. Armstrong had once told me about my Jordan outline—that I'd forgotten the most important thing.

"Can't have a great team," he said, "without great talent."

Pretty simple thought. But one of those things we have a tendency to forget. We think we can piece together our organizations with people of patchwork abilities, that we can stretch them to their absolute capacities and it will be enough.

And sometimes it may be.

But most of the time, it probably won't be.

You will notice that even the greatest coaches don't win without talent. When Phil Jackson first became coach of the Bulls, the franchise was just beginning to refine its talent level. When Jackson surrounded Jordan with a higher caliber of player, and with role players who completed their tasks without fail, the Bulls began to form a dynastic core.

"If you have talented players, you can win," Jackson said. "If you know what to do as a coach, you can bring out the best in talented players. To go off and coach a team that's going to win fifteen games, I can't."

It matters, of course, that you are able to recognize talent ("The ability to discover ability in others," said author Elbert Hubbard, "is the true test"), and to choose coachable people, those who are willing to accept the demands of others, who are dedicated to goals larger than themselves.

It also matters that you help talent settle into its proper place. The key to handling talent, says sports executive Mark McCormack, is this: "Employ it properly, then leave it alone."

"Find some people who are 'comers,'" said Dallas businessman John Stemmons. "People who are going to be achievers in their own field and people you can trust. Then grow old together." NBA player Juwann Howard asks, "You know how good teams win? By staying together."

> *Talent alone is not enough. They used to tell me you have to use your five best players, but I've found that you win with the five who fit together best.*
> —Red Auerbach

And this is what Bulls general manager Jerry Krause did. He drafted Horace Grant and Scottie Pippen in the spring of 1987, then hired Jackson as an assistant coach (under Doug Collins) that fall. He recruited the best talent he could find. He set the pieces into place. It was up to Jackson to provide for the development of his young players, like Pippen, a raw talent from Central Arkansas. Jackson taught him to find his shot and to harness his athleticism, to develop his abilities in four crucial dimensions: physical strength and skill, plus emotional and spiritual well-being.

So the talent was acquired, and the talent was harnessed. It was up to Jordan to provide the final element: cohesion.

"Michael had four qualities," said NBA scout Yvan Kelly. "Number one—superior athletic ability; number two—superior skills; number three—mental toughness; and number four—synthesizing these elements into team play. You will find players with as much talent and skills, but they just can't pull it together."

## 2. Leadership

*There are many elements to a campaign. Leadership is number one. Everything else is number two.*

—BERTOLT BRECHT
*business leader*

Here is another word that has infused itself into nearly every facet of the corporate lexicon—leadership. In fact, barely a day passes that my mailbox is not stuffed with an invitation to a seminar or conference on leadership. One of these took me to Grand Rapids, Michigan, where the Magic leadership group spent two days going through team-building exercises, including an afternoon in the woods doing team adventure drills. Our final activity of the day: climbing a twenty-five-foot wooden wall.

The rules were that two people could help from a platform stationed at the top, but no one else. This meant the first and last people had to get up without help.

There were eighteen of us. It took thirty minutes. When we were finished, we celebrated as if we'd just won an NBA championship.

Of course, it didn't hurt having our team vice president, Julius Erving, climb up that wall in two giant strides to complete the drill.

> *Leadership is getting players to believe in you.*
> —Larry Bird

In the midst of the 1992–93 season, the Bulls were struggling through a long road trip and trailing Utah by seventeen points in the waning seconds of the third quarter when Jordan hit a half-court shot to cut the lead to fourteen. Suddenly, something triggered. "Michael became so driven, so focused, so committed to his teammates," said former Bull Trent Tucker.

In the fourth quarter, Jordan scored twenty-two points. Chicago won the game.

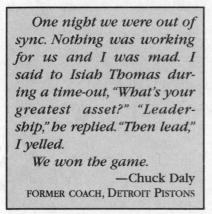

*One night we were out of sync. Nothing was working for us and I was mad. I said to Isiah Thomas during a time-out, "What's your greatest asset?" "Leadership," he replied. "Then lead," I yelled.*

*We won the game.*

—Chuck Daly
FORMER COACH, DETROIT PISTONS

So important is this concept that I've dedicated the entire next chapter (chapter 9) to it. But the obvious relationship between leadership and teamwork is this: *Every team needs its leaders.* There are certainly varied types of leaders, some who lead through action and some who lead more vocally.

Michael Jordan, at times, could be both.

"MJ had an ability to orchestrate a game," said NBA assistant coach Jim Eyen. "He was a maestro. He couldn't do it by himself, so he'd delegate, but he was always in control of the baton. He learned how to make other players feel part of what he was doing."

"During the 1991 finals," said former Bulls'

> *You have achieved excellence as a leader when people will follow you anywhere, if only out of curiosity.*
> —General Colin Powell

assistant John Bach, "MJ got up and told the team, 'Look, we're going to the top. You're either with me or you're not.'"

The night before training camp was due to begin, Phil Jackson would ask around the room, soliciting from each player his individual goals. Back came the answers: points, rebounds, assists, an All-Star game appearance. Jordan would always go last. He would always say the same thing.

> *Visions are never the sole property of one man or one woman. Before a vision can become reality, it must be owned by every single member of the group.*
> —Phil Jackson

"I have no individual goals," he said. "We play for one reason and that's to win the title. Practice is more important than the games, and I will practice when I'm hurt, when 95 percent of the players in this league would sit out. I expect all of you to do the same thing. You will follow my lead."

And follow they did.

## 3. Commitment

*"Individual commitment to a group effort; that is what makes a team work, a company work, a society work, a civilization work."*

—Vince Lombardi

## Commitment to the Team

By never demanding a trade, by refusing to bail out on the team that drafted him, Jordan first displayed the depth of his commitment to the Bulls. What he needed were players around him who were willing to make the same sacrifice, to subordinate themselves to a singular vision. That took time. People like this, who are willing to collectively pursue a goal or a vision, who are willing to hold to their promises in the face of adversity, are not easy to find. But they are worth searching for. "No team has ever achieved extraordinary results without a 100 percent commitment to the cause," said author John Maxwell.

> *When you're interested in something you do it only when it's convenient. When you're committed to something, you accept no excuses, only results.*
>
> —Kenneth Blanchard
> AUTHOR

Businessman Richard Edler found such a person. "One day in the office of the chairman of the company, I noticed a picture of his college board of directors. In the center was an elderly man badly hunched over. My chairman explained that he was the president. When he was a young man he played the piano professionally with great love, then he suffered an accident that broke his back. The doctors gave him a choice. He could have his back set permanently straight like everybody else, but he would never again play the piano or he could have his back set hunched over, allowing him to play but never stand up again. He chose the piano. I am not sure I would have, but I deeply admire his commitment to something."

## Commitment to Quality and Excellence— to Winning

Phil Jackson crafted a system. He knew he had to in order to get the rest of the team to commit, to adhere, to believe. What he adopted, in the 1989–90 season, was assistant Tex Winter's complex triple-post, or triangle, offense. It was not something that Jordan committed to immediately.

"There is no 'I' in team," Winter once said.

"There is in win," Jordan replied.

It was a difficult system, and it meant Jordan had to share the ball, to trust his teammates, to allow them their shots. But gradually, the Bulls adhered, and by midseason, they won twenty-four of twenty-seven games and began the process of eclipsing their nemesis, the Detroit Pistons. Jordan and Jackson began to forge a relationship that would become indelible. And Jordan began the process of instilling faith in his teammates.

"I tried to make him understand that to win a championship, he had to share the ball," Jackson said. "He had to share the limelight. He had to share some of the glory."

The triangle offense became the staple of the Bulls' championship teams. So did players like Pippen and Grant, like John Paxson and Steve Kerr, like Will Perdue and Bill Wennington.

"In Chicago, we knew what we had to do to win, and

> *I always felt that in order for a team to win you have to make the weakest link strong.*
>
> —Oscar Robertson
> NBA LEGEND

that was play together," said Horace Grant. "On the court, you have to be one unit. When you play with Michael Jordan, you have to put your ego aside. He was the man. With me, that was not difficult at all. I love winning championships."

## Commitment to Continual Improvement; to Hustling and Finishing

The Bulls had lost twelve of their last thirteen games in Detroit when they went to play the Pistons in mid-season in 1991. They won that game, 95–93, and it was as if, finally, the albatross of the Pistons had been shed. Later, the Bulls swept the Eastern Conference finals against Detroit in four games, with Jordan's aggressiveness setting the tone.

Perhaps the defining moment of that series, a prime example of the Bulls' heightened hustle, came on a Vinnie Johnson steal in Game Three. Jordan chased him down from behind and Johnson slowed up to let Jordan fly past. But somehow, Jordan adjusted himself, forcing Johnson to throw up a weak shot that Jordan rebounded. The Pistons were never close again. The Bulls were the dominant team in the NBA. They had mastered the triangle; more importantly, they had mastered each other.

## Commitment to Self-Discipline

"I didn't want to give up, no matter how sick I was, or how tired I was, or how low on energy I was," Jordan said. "I felt the obligation to my team, to the city of Chicago, to go out and give that extra effort. . . ."

> *A man is only as good as what he loves.*
> —Saul Bellow
> WRITER

## 4. Passion

*Vision is the stuff of our dreams. Passion is the energy to make it real. The two go together, like a horse and a rider. In the mind of one is the goal. In the power of the other lies the means to get there.*

—PETER URS BENDER
*author*

We discussed it in chapter 2, but it is worth reiterating here. It was Jordan's passion that drove the Bulls. He urged his teammates to hone their game, to practice every day without flagging and without succumbing to injury. He was the one setting the example. His feelings had a way of bubbling to the surface in fits of fury and rage and even sadness. And yet they often proved fruitful. They were the manifestation of Jordan's intense feeling for the game, a heightened sense of purpose that affected the entire franchise.

When Rodney McCray joined the Bulls, he brought his reputation with him. He was a stats guy, playing for num- bers, and Jordan wouldn't tolerate it.

> *The world belongs to the energetic.*
> —Ralph Waldo Emerson

"The first day of camp," said John Bach, the ex-Bulls assistant, "MJ goes up to him and says, 'I know all about you. But we're not like that here. We play hard. We play for the team. And I'm going to take you every day in practice, so you know what I'm talking about.'"

"Michael was a great finisher," said Kirk Champion, the Birmingham pitching coach when Jordan played minor-league baseball. "He had such passion for driving in runs or stealing a base, something that would help the team succeed. He really took pride in picking up that run from third base. He had a passion to finish and go after people."

## 5. Team Thinking

*The point was for the Celtics to win. Always. Not last week. Not next year. Right now. If I play well, that's one thing, but to make others play better . . . you understand what I mean? The game was scheduled, we had to play it, so we might as well win.*

—BILL RUSSELL
*ex-Celtics center*

"No team understood better than the Bulls that selflessness is the soul of teamwork," Phil Jackson said. "They plugged into the power of oneness, instead of the power of one man, and transcended the divisive forces of the ego that have crippled far more gifted teams. Michael was willing to sacrifice some of his own game for the rest of them. That was the most important thing he did."

## The Requirements of Team Thinking— *Be Unselfish*

There is a word for it in Japan, one that circulates among Japanese baseball players. The word is "Wa."

In America, there is no single word for it. It is a concept: Subordinating your needs for the good of the team.

"The team itself," Phil Jackson said, "must be the leader of the team."

## Find a Role and Fill It

Steve Kerr. John Paxson. Bill Cartwright. Bill Wennington. Luc Longley. Scott Williams. . . .

We could go on here. The point is, the Bulls had dozens of role players who helped them win six championships. Each had their moment. "My goal," Jackson said, "was to give everyone on the team a vital role and

> *There's nothing worse than an all-star band with no teamwork.*
> —Les Brown
> BANDLEADER

inspire them to be acutely aware of what was happening—even when the spotlight was on somebody else. Coaching is winning players over and convincing them they have to play together."

"We knew we had responsibilities," Jordan said, "and we knew our capabilities."

## Be a Team of Cheerleaders

"Accept a loss as a learning experience," Jordan said, "and never point fingers at your teammates."

## Have Fun

I learned this from my mentor in sports management, Bill Veeck. No one had more fun than Veeck. Wackiness was a prerequisite for a job in

Veeck's front office. Now Veeck's son, Mike, is running a minor-league baseball club, and on his door is a sign:

It says: "FUN IS GOOD."

Here's a little formula that works everytime: Choose to have fun. Fun creates enjoyment. Enjoyment invites participation. Participation focuses attention. Attention expands awareness. Awareness promotes insight. Insight generates knowledge. Knowledge facilitates action. Action yields results. And it all started by choosing to have fun.

### Follow the Leader

"MJ had a selfishness within the selflessness," said NBA Hall of Famer Julius Erving. "It's a fine line you have as a star—how many shots a game are too many? You need to score big to win, but how do your teammates react? It's a very delicate balancing act. Phil Jackson understood that with Michael and helped him balance being a dominant force and including the other guys."

"Michael had unique communication skills," said former NBA player Charles Smith. "He could communicate with his teammates and earn their respect. He could communicate with coaches and earn their respect. And he could communicate with owners and earn their respect. By doing this, Michael created a sense of community."

### Be Flexible

"There's a misconception about teamwork," said Hall of Fame football coach Tom Landry. "Teamwork is the ability to have different thoughts about things; it's the ability to argue and stand up and say loud and strong what you feel, but in the end, it's also the ability to adjust to what is best for the team."

"The way to tap into energy," Phil Jackson said, "is not by being autocratic, but by working with the players and giving them increasing responsibility to shape their roles."

### Think In Sync

This was a memo handed to the Magic players before the 2000–01 season:

#### Teammates Are Forever

The ones you practice with, spend time with, all but live with. The ones who become such a big part of your life, regardless of how the team does. Like men who have been to war together, teammates share things that no one else can really understand or fully appreciate. As if they have been members of some exclusive club, complete with its own codes and secrets.

## Be Consistent

"Once I asked Michael what he was thinking about when he took the final shot in Game Six in 1998," said Jordan's business partner and Washington Capitals owner Ted Leonsis. "Michael said, 'I wasn't thinking about anything because I'd taken that shot a million times in practice. If I hadn't taken that shot a million times, I would have had something to think about.'"

In the May 28, 2001 *ESPN* magazine, Jordan made this revealing statement:

"The ability to perform in the clutch comes from having the confidence to know that you can. Where does that confidence come from? From having done it in the past. Of course, you have to do it that first time, but after that, you've got a model you can always relate back to. It gives you comfort doing something you've done before.

> *For decades, great ath-*
> *letic teams have harbored*
> *one simple secret that only*
> *a few select business teams*
> *have discovered. It is this: To*
> *play and win together, you*
> *must practice together.*
> —Lewis Edwards
> BUSINESSMAN

What it gets down to is confidence and pride. Confidence is based in having done it before. There were days when I didn't want to work out, practice, whatever, but I did because I don't want that next guy catching me. That's why, if the game is tied in the last two minutes or down the stretch, I feel I have an advantage over everyone."

Wayne Gretzky said, "No matter who you are, no matter how good an athlete you are, we're creatures of habit. The better your habits are, the better they'll be in pressure situations."

### 6. Empowering Individuals

*"The magic of MJ was that he got everyone on the team to think that the Bulls won because of them—that they were the missing link."*
—BILL WALTON
*Hall of Fame player and broadcaster*

What changed when Jordan incorporated his game into a team concept is that he began to look around more often. He stopped cutting down his teammates in the newspaper, and he started to rely on them, to build trust and respect (something we will also explore in chapter 10). When he was double- and triple-teamed, he found his open teammates. He passed them the ball and put the pressure on them to make their shots. If they did, he found them again. He encouraged them. When the Bulls came out sluggish in one of the NBA Finals games against Utah, Steve Kerr missed his first shot. The next time down, Kerr passed up an open look. Jordan yelled at him, "Take the shot."

Kerr made his next one.

It is worth noting that Kerr was one of Jordan's most intense "motivational" projects. In fact, Jordan was so tough on Kerr that he once picked a fight with him during practice. But when it mattered, they trusted each other.

"MJ would include his teammates in the game early," Walton said, "then bail them out in the fourth quarter when it was winning time."

Craig Hodges, Michael's former teammate, has a vivid memory of that happening: "In the 1989 play-offs with Cleveland, I'll never forget the famous 'Ehlo Game.' The Cavs scored in the closing seconds, and the defensive mistake was mine. I felt I'd cost us the game and at the time-out MJ could feel my pain. He said to me, 'Don't even worry about it, Hodge. I've got you covered.' Then he hits the miracle shot to win it for us. I was off the hook. What a teammate."

In a couple of those championship seasons, it wasn't even Jordan who hit the winning shot; instead it was Jordan who drew the defense and passed off to either John Paxson or Steve Kerr for the final blow. For both men, solid but unspectacular guards, it was the moment that defined their careers. And it was a result of the confidence that Jordan instilled in them—something that Kerr had a little fun with during a victory parade speech after his shot won the title in 1997.

Here, Kerr told the crowd, was what "really happened" during that final time-out before his game-winning shot:

"Phil Jackson told Michael to take the last shot. Michael said he didn't really 'feel comfortable in these situations' and that maybe the Bulls should go 'in a different direction.' So, I thought to myself, *I guess I have to bail Michael out again. But why not? I've been bailing him out all season.*"

This is, of course, the extremely exaggerated

version of how Jordan affected his teammates. But somewhere within in Kerr's false braggadocio lies the truth. When Jordan showed he was on your side, when he helped you off the floor after a hard

> *Trust each other, again and again. When the trust level gets high enough, people transcend apparent limits, discovering new and awesome abilities for which they were previously unaware.*
> —David Armistead
> AUTHOR

foul and whispered in your ear, "Don't let them know you're hurt," there was a tendency to believe you could do anything.

"Creating a successful team," said Phil Jackson, "is essentially a spiritual act."

Jackson is a renowned believer in Zen and meditation and other esoteric concepts, but this notion is not grounded in any kind of complex Eastern philosophy. The spirituality of it—as it is within any group situation, athletic, corporate, or otherwise—is this: to surrender egotism in favor of altruism. To develop a network of employees, of teammates, who trust each other enough to believe that any of them could close the deal.

"Respect, dignity and integrity," Jordan said, "haven't gone out of style."

## 7. Build Trust and Respect

(see chapter 10)

## 8. Build and Model Character

*"Your ethical muscle grows stronger every time you choose right over wrong. Your character is your destiny."*

—PRICE PRITCHETT
*businessman*

This notion (explored more fully in chapter 11) was instilled in Jordan at North Carolina, a place where great sacrifices were met with great rewards. The more you sacrificed, the more it came to mean. That which came easily would never be valued. "The ethic (at North Carolina)," wrote David Halberstam, "seemed to come from another time."

It is a notion that springs from John Wooden's era. And it is a notion that has become lost somewhere in a dusty corner as professional sports have burgeoned.

"While individual athletes have gotten better over the years, without a doubt, team play has, in fact, declined," said Wooden, who won ten NCAA Championships at UCLA in the 1960s and 1970s.

Perhaps it's the media attention, perhaps it's the money, perhaps it's the overwhelming cult of celebrity, but as that acceptance of sacrifice and teamwork has declined, so has the general character of the modern athlete. Today's superstars are arrogant enough to believe that they can win on their own; early in the 2000–01 NBA season, Shaquille O'Neal and Kobe Bryant immersed themselves in a feud that threatened to tear apart Phil Jackson's newest potential dynasty, the Los Angeles Lakers.

"The real leader of that team," Jordan said of the Shaq/Kobe dispute, "is the one who can sacrifice and step back and let the other one be the leader." Of course, the Lakers did resolve their problems and rolled to their second straight NBA title in June of 2001.

Even now, as he works to improve the Washington Wizards, Jordan will remind his employees in team meetings on marketing and promotion and other business that "everything is a team sport."

That Jordan was able to recognize the value of the team is one of a myriad of reasons why his example should be cherished. For all of his flaws, Jordan was consistently able to recognize what

was best for the greater good. The optimal teammates are those who do the right thing, those
who have honesty and integrity, who share a
strong work ethic and a sense of maturity and
responsibility and self-discipline, who display perseverance and humility and courage. They are destined to become the crucial cogs in a machine,
one that grinds in endless pursuit of something
bigger than any individual could ever accomplish.

# CHAPTER NINE

# THE EYES UPON YOU

**JORDAN ON LEADERSHIP:**

I can't live up to the expectations people have of me. They're exaggerated. But I have my own expectations as a leader. . . . That's what I can live up to.

*I have it, but I'll be darned if I can define it.*

—General George Patton
on leadership

e're in the midst of a leadership crisis. Or at least that's what they tell me. I speak to executives and coaches and managers, and this is their lament—that there is a dearth of gifted young leaders. And so it's become trendy to hold leadership conferences, to share divergent theories about leadership, to put heads together and attempt to analyze and isolate the problem.

Do I have the answers to all of these issues? Of course not. But I can say that we in the NBA have seen this leadership problem affect us firsthand. Our league is floundering right now, ticket sales and television ratings are plummeting, the luster of our star players is fading, the popularity of the league is on a downward slide. The truth is, we didn't know how good we had it when Michael Jordan was around (and before Jordan, Julius Erving, Magic Johnson and Larry Bird). As much as I credit David Stern and others in the NBA front office for the boom in popularity of the NBA, none of them was our acknowledged leader.

Michael was our leader.

He was the one in the commercials, the one in the promotions, the one on the magazine covers. He was our representative image. Michael sold jerseys and Michael sold hats and Michael sold tickets, and produced TV ratings which, as any half-witted sports executive will tell you, is the only thing that matters. Michael was very much aware of this undeniable truth.

And Michael did not just sell tickets in Chicago. Michael sold tickets in New York and Cleveland and Milwaukee and Los Angeles. I once spoke to a businessman in Oakland—and I'm sure there are dozens of stories like this—who said his company bought season tickets to Golden State Warriors games in order to have their corporate box available for one game—against the Bulls.

Michael's game.

> It's impossible to have any success as a quarterback without being a leader, since all eyes in the huddle will be on you. If you're uncertain about things, your teammates will know.
>
> —Joe Montana

"Michael had a special ability to lead others because he thought about the game all the time and understood it," said former NBA coach Mike Fratello. "He didn't just go out and play. He was always anticipating what could happen next, and how he could get his teammates involved."

So as the NBA's popularity peaked in the '90s, we in pro basketball's front offices began to congratulate ourselves. *Boy,* we thought, *are we good.* We genuflected upon packed arenas and boisterous crowds. We restocked the gift shop and ordered a few thousand more hot dogs.

And then Michael retired for good. And here we are, without a spokesman, without a voice, without a leader. Every time someone steps forward, he appears to shun the role or to stumble in some way. And the NBA remains a league without a pacesetter.

Certainly, these are enormous shoes to fill, but our most effective leaders are able to shoulder great burdens. Our most effective leaders share certain qualities.

## 1. Vision

*Great leaders are visionaries. They have an instinct for the future ... a course to steer ... a port to seek. For persuasion, they win the consent of their people.*

—ARTHUR SCHLESINGER JR.
*historian*

*Woodrow Wilson had the ability to see around the corners, to see the future before it's here.*

—Bill Bradley
U.S. SENATOR

Vision is not something that can be explained as much as it can be signified. True vision is more than just adherence to the typical rules of success. It is more than just setting goals. It is a transcendent sense of meaning and purpose, the radiant desire that you recognize in someone as soon as you see it. ("Vision leaks," said pastor and author Bill Hybels.)

Visionaries are the ones we defer to in times of crisis. They share ideas that are easily understood, that are attainable, yet are only seen in their entirety by the rarest of people. ("Vision," said author Jonathan Swift, "is the art of seeing the invisible.") Visionaries focus others around their plan, keep others fueled and are driven to complete the entire picture of their vision without quitting when things become difficult.

Visionaries are the people who we say were meant to lead.

"I had a long conversation with Michael Jordan, and he broke it down to a science," said Minnesota Timberwolves forward Kevin Garnett. "He told me about coming out each night and setting a tone with your play, both on offense

and defense. Being
ready. Taking that
next step. He told
me a lot of key

> *Vision without action is a daydream. Action without vision is a nightmare.*
> —Japanese Proverb

things that you'd think you would know, but it's
not always the case. Killer-instinct stuff. Use your
instincts. Be aggressive and if the team's not following you, you have to be that leader to push
the team over the hump. Mike's sort of a deep
guy. . . . You want to tape record when he talks, so
you remember a lot of stuff."

## 2. Communication Skills

*Ninety percent of leadership is the ability to communicate something people want.*

—DIANE FEINSTEIN
*U.S. Senator*

There was a year when the Bulls split their
first two home play-off games with the Atlanta
Hawks. What happened after the Bulls lost Game
Two is an example of Jordan, the communicator,
at his most potent: he got in everyone's face. His
message was rather simple and quite straightfor-
ward. He said, "This will never happen again. We
must win this."

You could call this "fiery optimism." It is the foremost quality of an effective communicator.

"You had no chance after that," Bulls assistant coach Frank Hamblen would tell Hawks assistant Stan Albeck later that summer.

And he was right. The Bulls won the series.

"MJ," Albeck said, "would not let you lose."

Michael Jordan was an inspirational leader. Businessman Robert Mondavi understands that: "Out of all the rigidities and mistakes of my past, I've learned one final lesson, and I'd like to see it engraved on the desk of every business leader, teacher and parent in America—the greatest leaders don't rule. They inspire."

"Michael was a quiet leader at the start," said former Bulls trainer Mark Pfeil, "but as the years went by, he became more vocal and took charge."

> *I am an optimist. It does not seem too much use being anything else.*
> —Winston Churchill

"In 1995, the Magic beat us in the play-offs in six games, so when we played them again in 1996, it was big," said former Bull Jack Haley. "In Game One, we blew them out, but in Game Two, they jumped all over us in the first half. At the half, you could see the fear and hesitation in our faces. Michael stands up and says, 'Trust in me. Climb up on my back and let me carry you. I'll take care of the rest.' You could feel the goose bumps after that. We won the game and we swept the series."

What else must great communicators rely on besides optimism?

They must be storytellers, like Phil Jackson, who is known to quote scripture and Zen literature to his players in a way that they can understand. And they must gauge the

> *If one had to name a single, all-purpose instrument of leadership, it would be communication.*
> —John W. Gardner
> AUTHOR

perceptions of their subjects, so that what's being said actually gets implemented. "It's about finding a level of confidence," Jackson said, "so that when they hear your voice, they know whose voice it is and it's the only voice speaking."

Communicators must also be attentive listeners. Phil Jackson's own theories for "mindful leadership" include this suggestion:

"Listen without judgment—no matter what the stakes and the situation, practice listening with impartial, open awareness. Key on your team members' body language and the silence between words. As a result, you will better understand their concerns and receive improved performance."

This is something that Jordan abided by as well. As difficult and demanding as he could be, the way he learned how to give his teammates that extra push, how to motivate each of them most effectively, was by paying attention to their needs, to what they responded to most effectively. "My role as a leader was to help them find different types of challenges," Jordan said.

By the time he was finished, Jordan could communicate without speaking, with one look, one glare across the dressing room at a player he felt was taking a night off. "Coming from a guy who never took a night off," said John Bach, "that would get you going. Michael was never a Salvation Army worker . . . the guy who was going to solve everyone's problems, or fix everything in the world. But he picked the times that were important."

Motivational speaker Brian Tracy hit it right on the nose when he said, "The world is full of people who are waiting for someone to come along and motivate them to be the kind of people they wish they could be. . . . These people are waiting for a bus on a street where no busses pass."

Communicators must also be relaxed public speakers. This is something that perhaps did not come naturally to Jordan, but it became instilled in him over time, and he blossomed into one of the league's most eloquent spokesmen.

Lastly, communicators must adhere to their own thinking above all else. They have to assert themselves, their own beliefs, and do it in their own way. For Jordan, this was often done without a great deal of verbalization.

"I was never one of those vocal, rah-rah types of guys," he said. "I may have given some vocal leadership, but that rah-rah stuff was immature to a certain extent. I was not the person to do that."

## 3. People Skills

*I don't think people are going to be successful on whether they nail the technology. They are going to be successful if they nail the sociology.*

—LEE DINGEL
*business executive*

Here again, it was Jackson who set the standard for the Bulls by treating his players with maturity and respect. "With Phil," said NBA veteran John Salley, "it's, 'You're a man. I'm a man. I'm going to help you be a better man.' Phil understands people." I like the Liberian proverb that says, "If the townspeople are happy, look for the chief."

Jackson was a teacher, a coach, a friend, a counselor. He was visible and he was available. He concerned himself with the welfare of every one of his players, both on and off the court. He encouraged and he listened. He did not exaggerate mistakes—"My attitude is, 'I know you made a mistake, and the rest of the team knows you made a mistake . . . but it's not personal criticism,'" Jackson said—and he balanced his criticism with compliments.

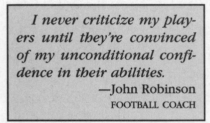

> *I never criticize my players until they're convinced of my unconditional confidence in their abilities.*
> —John Robinson
> FOOTBALL COACH

"Compassionate leadership," Jackson called it—in other words, treating

> *Most of us can run pretty well all day long on one compliment.*
> —Mark Twain

people with the same respect and care you'd give to yourself. Using your authority sparingly. Allowing room for a sense of humor.

"Phil let us be our own people," Jordan said. "But within a structure."

It was something else that rubbed off on Jordan.

"He's encouraging with the guys, trying to tell them what to do, where he'll be on the court. 'You set this pick, then I'll use you that way.' That kind of stuff," said Bulls coach Phil Jackson on Jordan's career transformation. "He's taking guys and playing one-on-one, players like Dickey Simpkins, for the fun and thrill of it. He's still involved in the shooting games and likes to make those little bets, but there's also been this acceptance, which has helped us as coaches."

"Michael had an attitude toward us of protection," Trent Tucker said. "He basically said, 'I must take care of these eleven guys so that when the battle hits they'll be strong enough to take care of themselves.' That's what a leader does."

Los Angeles writer J. A. Adande saw Jordan's leadership skill in action: "In 1993, the Bulls won

> *Red Auerbach told me early on, whenever a player asks for some time off because of a wedding, birth, illness, whatever, give it to him. Give him a little extra, and he'll always pay you back with a little extra when he comes back.*
> —Rick Pitino
> FORMER CELTICS COACH

their third straight title. However, they got a scare in the Conference Finals when New York won the first two at home. The Bulls won Game Three and just before the Bulls took the floor to start Game Four, I saw Michael in the hall outside the locker. He was dancing in front of his teammates with three fingers in the air and singing enthusiastically, 'Three-peat, three-peat.' I thought *What confidence he has* and how must that make his teammates feel."

In the 1993 finals, the Bulls led the series 3–1 before losing Game Five at home to Phoenix. The Bulls were stunned. The city of Chicago had been braced for a celebration. Instead, it was back to Phoenix for Game Six.

> *I decided I was going to become an optimist, when I decided I wasn't going to win anymore games by being anything else.*
> —Earl Weaver
> HALL OF FAME MANAGER

The next day at the airport, the team was tight. They waited for Jordan to show. He was the last one there. He strutted onto the plane with a huge cigar in his mouth.

"What's this?" asked Bulls owner Jerry Reinsdorf.

"My victory cigar," he said.

On the plane, Jordan spoke one-on-one with every player. He started a massive card game. By the time the plane landed, the team was loose again.

The Bulls won Game Six to finish off their third consecutive title.

This people skills story touched the Williams family deeply. My son Bobby has had a passion for baseball from the time he discovered that baseballs are round. He worked diligently to hone his catching skills with the dream of becoming a major leaguer. In 1999, he graduated from Rollins College, where he was a backup catcher on the varsity baseball team.

Bobby realized that his dreams of going to the big show as a player would not become a reality. Jim Bowden, general manager of the Cincinnati Reds, and also a Rollins graduate, learned of Bobby's baseball knowledge and love of the game and hired him, at age twenty-two, to be a first-base coach for the Reds' Billings Mustangs minor-league team, making Bobby the youngest coach ever in professional baseball history.

The Reds' first spring training game of 2001 was coincidentally scheduled to be played at Rollins. The night before the game Bowden and Reds' skipper, Bob Boone, contacted Bobby at training camp in Sarasota and told him to be dressed and ready to coach first base for the Reds.

The bus rolled into the Rollins stadium. Manager Boone walked off, followed by Ken Griffey, Jr., Barry Larkin, Deion Sanders, and Bobby Williams! The people skills of Bowden and Boone provided a major-league thrill for Bobby Williams (and his dad) that day.

### 4. Character

*There is, in our day, only one kind of strength which is lasting—it is that proceeding from character.*

—ALEXIS DE TOCQUEVILLE
*historian*

General Norman Schwarzkopf is a true American hero because of his strong stand on the importance of character. He stated, "The main ingredient of good leadership is good character. This is because leadership involves conduct, and conduct is determined by values."

Character is a product of humility and integrity, of possessing the confidence to adapt to certain situations, as Jordan displayed in the 1992 Olympics and as Scottie Pippen did not in the 1994 play-offs.

For all of Jordan's apparent flaws, his

recognition of these qualities—especially within the team dynamic—was unflinching. Sportswriter Jackie McMullan visited Jordan in Birmingham during his stint in baseball. It was the day after Pippen, feeling disrespected and petulant, had refused to play in the final minutes of a play-off game in 1994.

"Can you believe that?" Jordan said.

"No," McMullan replied. "Can you believe it?"

"Those guys," Jordan said, "never realized what it takes to be a leader."

"The 1992 Olympics were dominated by the Dream Team, and Michael Jordan was the dominant player on the team," said *Sports Illustrated* writer Jack McCallum. "However, MJ stepped back and let Magic Johnson run the show and be the team leader. MJ sensed that Magic was better than him at this function, and it would be best for the team if Magic had the lead role."

> *Integrity is everything. Without it, you go nowhere and lead no one.*
> —Dennis McDermott
> AUTHOR

## 5. Competence

*Leaders are made, not born. They are made by hard effort, which is the price which all of us must pay to achieve any goal that is worthwhile.*

—VINCE LOMBARDI

"MJ had the rare knack to be a great leader. He just outworked everybody," said Brad Daugherty, a Cleveland Cavaliers center and Jordan's North Carolina teammate. "He'd be the first and last in the weight room, on the floor—it didn't matter. He just had the drive to outwork you. I learned about work ethic from Michael. He took me aside and gave me a lot of confidence. He'd stay on me. He'd compliment you if you did what you were meant to be doing and not the extra. He just expected you to do that."

Jordan demanded a great deal, but he'd earned that right. He was the franchise, the nucleus, and he'd proven himself. This is what we mean by competence: a strong track record. "You don't become a leader because you say you are," said former Detroit Tigers manager Sparky Anderson. "It's much more what you do than what you say." Jockey Willie Shoemaker stated, "The horse never knows I'm there until he needs me."

"It's hard to lead unless you're demanding of yourself," said former NBA coach John Calipari. "You can't demand anything of others until you've shown that you're willing to do it yourself. That's why MJ was a great leader."

The other facet of establishing your competence is a commitment to continual growth. For Jordan, that meant studying the opposition, educating himself on the nuances of the NBA.

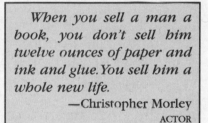

> *When you sell a man a book, you don't sell him twelve ounces of paper and ink and glue. You sell him a whole new life.*
> —Christopher Morley
> ACTOR

For the rest of us, it means reading and thinking and learning—both in and out of our chosen field—long after our formal education is complete.

## 6. Boldness

*Boldness has genius, power and magic in it.*

—JOHANN WOLFGANG VON GOETHE
*writer*

Another of Phil Jackson's strengths as a coach was his encourage-ment of debate. He wanted people—his coaches, his players—to express their ideas, even if it exploded into an argument. He wanted everyone to feel free to speak, to empty their minds, to contribute experiences that may be unique to them. This led to better thought processes. And it bred a team that was willing to take risks—another attribute personified by both Jackson and Jordan.

"Above all, trust your gut," Jackson said. "This is the first law of leadership. Once you've made your move, you have to stand by your decision, and live with the consequences, because your number-one loyalty has to be to the team."

"When I was coaching at Boston College, we had a senior named Dana Barros," said college basketball coach Jim O'Brien. "Before the draft, a Bulls assistant coach called me about Dana. He asked, 'Would Barros have the ability as a point guard to wave off Michael when he comes off screens, yelling and demanding the ball?'

I said, 'No he doesn't. But I doubt your coaches do, either.'"

Back to Birmingham for a moment, to Jackie McMullan, who one night saw Jordan strike out

> *There is a tide in the affairs of men, which, taken at the flood, leads on to fortune; omitted, all the voyage of their life is bound in the shallows and in miseries ... and we must take the current when it serves, or lose our ventures.*
> —William Shakespeare

three times until, finally, a pinch hitter was called in to avoid embarrassment. Afterward, McMullan asked how he felt about it.

"I like the challenge," Jordan said. "The NBA is too easy for me."

Baseball, of course, was Jordan's ultimate risk. It was also a bold statement about the leadership qualities of a man who refused to listen to anyone who thought he should take the easy way out.

"You must forget about being cautious, because if you don't, you're licked before you start," Vince Lombardi said. "There is nothing to be afraid of, as long as you are aggressive, and keep going. Keep going and you will win."

Two more thoughts on boldness from successful football coaches. "Be right or wrong, but be decisive in your actions," says Brian Billick.

Chuck Knox adds: "Conservative coaches have one thing in common: they are all unemployed."

## 7. Being a Servant

*No man will make a great leader who wants to do it all himself or to get all the credit for doing it.*

—ANDREW CARNEGIE

"I remember Phil Jackson telling MJ that he had to trust his teammates," said former Bulls forward Horace Grant.

> *I am reminded of a saying we have in the Army: "Officers eat last!" Taking care of your soldiers is an act of stewardship.*
> —General Colin Powell

"Mike didn't go overboard, but he'd invite guys to his room to play cards, just enough to let them know what he was about. To be a leader, everybody has to have respect for you on and off the court. You can't just be a great player."

There is a well-documented incident that took place during the 1987–88 season, when Doug Collins was coaching the Bulls. Jordan came to practice in a bad mood. He was talking back to Collins. During a scrimmage, after a dispute over the score, Jordan unleashed a tirade on Collins.

"Would you say that to Dean Smith?" Collins asked.

"I'm leaving," Jordan said.

"We're not through for the day yet," Collins told him.

"I'm out of here," Jordan said.

He picked up his bag and he stormed out of practice. On the way out, Collins muttered, "Nice leadership, Michael."

It became a story for the media. It was reported and debated for a few days, until finally both men let it pass. But it was, Collins said, one of the first moments when Jordan recognized his impact, the magnitude of his stardom.

Later, Jordan came to Collins and assured him it would never happen again.

"I think this incident," Collins said, "was a turning point in his career."

* * *

Team players recognize the greater good. For Jordan, that meant adhering to a team dynamic, refusing to allow diversions and even controlling such unbridled personalities as Dennis Rodman. "Michael would not allow any diversions on that team," said former Dallas Mavericks general manager Norm Sonju. "He'd police that all by himself."

Sometimes, he even did it in the off-season. That summer in 1995, after Chicago lost to the Magic in the play-offs, the Bulls were gathering for informal practice sessions at ten in the morning every day. Some players would drift in later until, finally, Jordan grew tired of it and pulled his teammates into a huddle and said, "We're all professionals. If we say we're going to be here at ten, let's be here at ten." For the rest of the summer, that's what they did.

He was everything to the Bulls—a policeman, a catalyst, a communicator, a visionary. He carried a team. He carried an entire league. And of course he was unique; and of course he was incomparable. But I'm convinced that there are others out there who are willing to step forward, who are willing to shoulder the burdens that great leaders must bear.

It's up to us to find them. To develop them. And perhaps, to become them.

# CHAPTER TEN

# THE SOCIAL GENIUS

JORDAN ON RESPECT, TRUST AND LOYALTY:

I just think you should respect the game. Be positive people. Certainly, you can act like gentlemen and professionals. You look at the great players and what they want to pass on as a legacy. They don't take this game for granted. You don't treat it like dirt. We're being treated like doctors and lawyers because of the salaries we receive. So let's act like sensible people.

*Only those who respect others can be of real use to them.*

—Albert Schweitzer

his is a story from Birmingham, from 1994, when Michael Jordan was nothing more than another minor-league baseball player striving for an opportunity. It was a brilliant afternoon, warm and sunny, and he was on his way to the ballpark, cutting through a sprawling suburban neighborhood. He passed a boy, ten years old, playing basketball in his driveway, alone. The boy's name is not important. It could be any boy.

What matters is what the man did next.

He stopped the car. He got out. The boy considered him. The boy knew who he was.

"Mind if I join you?" Jordan asked.

The boy nodded.

They played for twenty minutes, passing, rebounding, shooting, the world's greatest basketball player and the boy, no one disturbing them. Then Jordan got in his car and drove away.

The boy's parents weren't home that afternoon.

When he told them, they didn't believe him. No one believed him. It was like something out of Grimm's Fairy Tales.

"Finally," said Birmingham Barons general manager Tony Ensor, "one of the neighbors verified his story."

> *At all of his camps, Michael Jordan will physically touch every camper. A hug, a pat, something. They all feel his touch.*
>
> —Dick Versace
> NBA EXECUTIVE

Here is the Michael Jordan we don't see. Here is what exists beyond the iconography. It is not a prepackaged smile, not a silhouetted T-shirt slogan, not a commercial spokesman, not a towering image on an IMAX screen.

No. Here is a man. And here is a child.

It could be any child. Say a nine-year-old with disfiguring burns. Or a teenager in a wheelchair who can move nothing except his eyes. Or a Make-A-Wish kid crippled by a rare and terminal disease. Or one of the perfectly healthy kids at his summer basketball camp. Or the son of an opposing coach. The point is, it does not matter.

What matters is what the man does next.

He hugs, he talks, he takes up twice the time allotted by the publicists and the agents for the Make-A-Wish children, until both of them are nearly in tears. ("This rips me up," he says when he's finished.) The parents see it and say, "That's the first time our child has smiled in three months." He talks to the kids about getting good grades, about respecting

> *A gentle word, a kind look, a good-natured smile, can work wonders and accomplish miracles.*
> —William Hazlitt
> AUTHOR

their parents. The parents come back and say their children's faces looked "like sunshine."

"MJ says he's going to give me his shoes tomorrow," one of the children says.

"Right, sure," thinks the parent, said an NBA assistant coach named T. R. Dunn.

The next day the parent is leaving the building and here's Jordan, passing him, saying, "Don't forget to get to the ball boy and get a pair of shoes for your son."

While at North Carolina, circa 1983, he plays a game of HORSE with a six-year-old boy who goes on to become an announcer in Knoxville, Tennessee. When the boy's mom comes to get him, she says, "Do you know who that was?"

"I had no idea I'd been playing with Michael Jordan," Deck Hardee says today.

In 1992, in a Chicago suburb, Jordan tells his driver to stop in front of some children who have set up a lemonade stand. He rolls down his window, buys some lemonade, talks with them and leaves. The children are so excited that they bowl over their entire operation.

The man is determined to do things like this. To pull a kid bedecked in Air Jordan wear out of the crowd to caddie for him at a celebrity golf tournament in Hilton Head, South Carolina. To open the gates of his house on Halloween for trick-or-treaters. To prove that he is something more than a shadowy logo on a T-shirt, more than a waggling tongue and a pair of legs scissoring through the free-throw lane. He notices the children with disadvantages, the shy ones who can't push their way up front, the kids in wheelchairs who can't get close. He picks them out. He crouches on the frozen ground until a disabled boy's father can take a photograph.

> *Michael Jordan was not good at saying no to people. He was known to stiff people, but they were always the powerful people. Michael always had an abundance of time for any person who was struggling, or who couldn't possibly be of any personal benefit to him.*
>
> —Bob Greene
> COLUMNIST

"My son still talks about it," one parent says.

"I have three sons," says NBA player Hersey Hawkins, "and every time MJ sees them, he remembers their names. That's amazing to me. Sometimes I can't even remember their names."

He has that kind of memory for faces, for names. He

sees a girl at his camp and winks and tells her, "You look much better now that your braces are off." He sees the same kid sneaking back into a massive line at an autograph session and says, "Isn't this your second time?" He meets Larry Johnson for the first time, when Johnson is a rookie forward in Charlotte, and asks him, "How's your mother? How's Dorothy?"

"I thought, 'How does he know my mother's name?'" Johnson said. "I thought about it the whole game."

He sees another rookie, Antonio Daniels, in a restaurant, and not only acknowledges him, but

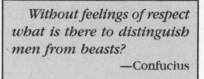

*Without feelings of respect what is there to distinguish men from beasts?*
—Confucius

invites him over to eat at his table. He sees a broadcaster, Jay Howard, who wore a line of Jordan's sweaters once, and from then on refers to him as "my sweater guy."

He has a keen awareness for the dynamics of family—his own and others. A fan in Indianapolis sees him in a department store, his arms loaded with stuffed animals, and when the fan asks who they're for, Jordan says, "Got to take care of my kids." One day in Aspen, a boy asks him to sign his brand-new ski jacket and Jordan says, "Does your mother know I'm signing this jacket?"

He ships a signed jersey to be buried with a dying boy

in Seattle. He donates thirty-five thousand dollars in auction proceeds to a foundation for a boy who died of brain cancer. He drives to a site near the old Chicago Stadium, in an inner-city neighborhood, where four boys wait on the corner to wave to him as he drives past. He nicknames one of them "Kool-Aid," and every night, he leaves four tickets for "Kool-Aid" at will-call. Sometimes they're seats upstairs, sometimes they're near courtside. Jordan always pays for them himself.

"MJ was always so aware of other people's feelings," said sportswriter Rick Telander. "He is a social genius."

One night in 1994, Birmingham plays a game at Nashville. The team bus is in centerfield, and Jordan is riding out to it on a golf cart, shrouded by security. A boy chases him. Security guards catch the boy and knock him down. This is not long after Monica Seles was stabbed during a tennis match, and no one is willing to take chances. The next day, the story comes out: The boy has a friend who died and who was a huge Jordan fan. The boy was sprinting out to invite Jordan to the funeral.

> *MJ taught me to respect what you do and do the right thing. Basketball is my profession, and Michael taught me to respect it.*
> —Derek Anderson
> NBA PLAYER

The man has to do something. And so he issues a statement: *I'm very sorry to hear of this tragic story.*

*I wish I could be at the funeral, but my baseball schedule will not permit it. My thoughts and prayers will be with the family at this time.*

"He always knew the right thing to say," said Chris Pika, Birmingham's publicist in 1994.

## "Did You Think I'd Be Late?"

"The sense of respect I get from the people—I get chill bumps," Jordan said. "Sometimes, I'm misty-eyed, and it doesn't have anything to do with whether it's a big game or not. It just happens."

It was respect that Jordan coveted. It is a simple equation: Respect between people leads to trust, and trust leads to loyalty, and it was my own mentor, Bill Veeck, who said, "For my dough, loyalty is the greatest virtue in the world."

"Sometimes, we forget what former NBA players did to allow us to come along today and earn the type of money we're making and gain the respect of fans and media," Jordan said. "I never want to forget that. That's the respect every athlete needs to pay back to the game."

And so Jordan's kindness was not just reserved for

children. It was given over to the entire league, to statisticians and ticket managers and trainers and custodians. It was given to opponents and to future opponents, like Carlos Rogers, a young player who went to a camp of Jordan's in Chicago before he came into the NBA. Rogers was swarmed by agents, talking to him, prodding him, and Jordan stepped in and screened them, told them they shouldn't talk to him and jeopardize his career.

"I didn't think a guy of that caliber would actually sit down with me in his office," said Rogers, "and tell me how to handle things."

He noticed. He was aware. He followed the league with a sharp eye so he could do little things like congratulate P. J. Brown on his new contract, so he could know each player by name and compliment them on their strengths. Was there gamesmanship involved, a sweetness to disguise the ruthlessness? Partly. But it wasn't just that.

"MJ had a great sense of his own legacy," said his Chicago teammate, Luc Longley.

"He could recognize people and read their character," said New York Knicks announcer John Andariese. "He had a great understanding of human nature."

When Ted Leonsis, Jordan's business partner, introduced him to his receptionist, she was speechless.

Then, as she took them on the elevator, she began to weep, and Jordan put his arm around her and comforted her.

He had a way of sensing the pulse of people, of knowing how to affect them. There was the Baskin-Robbins employee who, when she was told she was making a milkshake for Jordan after-hours one night, began to scream hysterically. A few minutes later, Leah Wilcox, an NBA employee who'd been sent for the shake, put her on the line to Jordan's room, and she screamed louder.

> *Once, when I was playing for Phoenix, I asked Michael for his shoes right in the middle of a game. After the game, he signed them and gave them to me.*
> —Steve Nash
> NBA PLAYER

There was Rogelio Nunez, a young Dominican catcher in Birmingham whom Jordan took a liking to. Told him to read the dictionary and study his English. Told him he'd give him a hundred dollars for every word he learned to spell. Before each game, Jordan would gather the team in a circle and Nunez would spell. By the end of the summer, Jordan had given away twelve hundred dollars, and at the end of the year, Jordan took Nunez to his house and gave him shoes, gloves, equipment, sweats, all straight out of his closet.

> *Establish, through every possible means, the self-respect of workers, and make them feel like they're part of the team, not just numbers on a time clock.*
> —C. Donald Dallas
> BUSINESSMAN

"In spring training, the players were complaining about the bus we'd have to ride in all summer," said Jordan's minor-league baseball teammate, Scott Tedder. "When we got to Birmingham, there were four buses waiting outside the ballpark. We looked at all four, and then MJ bought the one we wanted. After the season, he let the Barons keep it."

Tedder, Nunez's roommate in Birmingham, was released by the White Sox after a game in mid August of 1994. He was upset. He was confused. "MJ sat with me," Tedder said. "He talked to me. He explained why to me. He was really a friend."

The next day, the Cubs signed Tedder to play for their minor-league team in Orlando. They were playing at Birmingham. Problem was, Tedder didn't have any bats. He told the clubhouse boy to go tell Jordan. After batting practice, Tedder returned to his locker and found four of Jordan's bats waiting for him.

"Certain people or things seemed to strike Michael," said John Bach, the former Bulls assistant coach. "He had a charm about him, a special manner. He was never offended by people trying to get to him."

Carmen Villafane was a familiar face at Bulls games, a woman with severe disabilities, an invalid confined to a wheelchair. One year, before a game, she gave Jordan a valentine. A few months later, Jordan saw her at an auto show and asked her why she hadn't come to more games. She said she didn't have tickets, so Michael told her to call his office and he'd see what he could do.

Villafane called. Jordan's office mailed her tickets for the remainder of the season. The next season, Jordan sent her more tickets and a note that read, "I hope you enjoy the season ahead. I'm looking forward to seeing you at every game—Michael." Her wheelchair was positioned behind the bench at every game. When Jordan came back to Chicago for a Bulls-Wizards exhibition game in 2000, he visited with Carmen. He looked at her worn wheelchair and said, "I don't like this chair. We've got to get you a new one."

The next day, Jordan ordered it.

"The ultimate wheelchair," said Tim Floyd, who succeeded Phil Jackson as coach of the Bulls. "All the bells and whistles. Now she could ride in style."

There were no limits.

> *The most consistent lesson I've taught Shaq has been the value of respect. Always treat people as equals. The way you go up is the way you come down. When you come down, you come down a whole lot faster.*
> —Phillip Harrison
> SHAQUILLE O'NEAL'S FATHER

> *One night, a drunk woman wandered into Michael Jordan's hotel room to get his autograph while I was there. The woman acted like a bum. Michael treated her like she was Princess Diana.*
>
> —Lacy J. Banks
> SPORTSWRITER

Jordan even paid respect to the two entities who prove the nemesis of so many otherwise exemplary athletes: the referees and the media.

Joe Falls had been writing about sports for fifty years in Detroit. He was in his early seventies and he had never met Jordan before he played his final game in Detroit in 1993. When Falls got into the locker room, Jordan was the last one there.

"See this white hair?" Falls said. "You've got to talk to me."

Jordan grinned.

"I wanted to thank you," Falls said. "For all the times you talked to us after games. Whether you won or lost, you always had time to talk."

They shook hands. Falls left. He hadn't bothered to give his name.

A year later, Falls drove to the White Sox spring training camp to write a story on Jordan. A cluster of media had gathered at the front door of the clubhouse. Falls went around to the back to use the restroom. The door was open. When he walked in, the only other person in the room was Jordan.

"Joe Falls," he called. "What are you doing in here? Get over here."

Falls had never given his name. They had met only once. And yet that day Joe Falls got a private interview, slipped out the back door and went away.

"Can you believe that?" Falls said.

It's not as unusual as you might think. From the beginning, Jordan appealed to the media. The first time Mark Heisler of the *Los Angeles Times* came across Jordan was after the sixty-three-point game against the Celtics in the 1986 play-offs. *What a magnetic guy*, Heisler thought. He was never so conscious of wanting to know someone, of sensing an aura.

Oh, sure, they had their moments, Jordan and the media, as any public figure does in the face of such scrutiny. But there was something rare between Jordan and the reporters who covered him: an understanding, a symbiosis, a realization that each relied on the other to do their jobs properly. It was respectful. It was smart.

*Respect builds trust. Trust builds loyalty.*

"The writers may have wanted to write bad about Michael," said NBA player Tim Hardaway, "but they couldn't because MJ would win them over."

"I always feel like I have to pay my respect to you

guys—stupid questions and all," said Jordan, shortly after his last formal meeting with the press as a player. "I understood what dealing with the media was all about, and learning that was part of my education and maturity. I never wanted them to think of me as a rude type of guy."

"I was with Michael at least a hundred times," said columnist and author Terry Pluto. "He was never a jerk. He never blew me off. Was never rude. Didn't curse. Dressed well. He was always classy. He understood that he stood for something and had to act professionally. He was always gracious. He'd joke with you."

Sportswriters are not accustomed to being noticed by their subjects. And so when Jordan noticed Dallas writer David Moore leaving a Mexican restaurant and the next day asked him, "Did you enjoy dinner last night?" it made an impression. When Jay Mariotti wrote a pro-Jordan column in the *Chicago Sun-Times*, and the next day Jordan pulled him aside and said, "I appreciate that piece," it made an impression.

"He didn't have to do that," Mariotti said.

No, he didn't. He didn't have to extend his press conferences until the questions had trailed off, until everyone was satisfied. He didn't have to do the same interview with the same broadcaster, Mike O'Koren, twice in a row, after O'Koren's tape recorder failed to work the first time. He didn't have to answer each question thoughtfully, instead of resorting to pat responses and clichés. He didn't have to grant an interview to a reporter for a small golf newspaper the night before a game. And he didn't have to get dressed before the media was allowed in the locker room; it was a concession to the female reporters, of course, but also a dignified gesture from a man who is ever conscious of conducting himself properly.

> *A man who lies to himself and believes his own lies becomes unable to recognize truth, either in himself or anyone else, and he ends up losing respect for himself and others. When he has no respect for anyone, he can no longer love, and in order to divert himself, having no love in him, he yields to his impulses, indulging in the lowest form of pleasure, and behaves, in the end, like an animal, in satisfying his vices. It all comes from lying ... lying to others and lying to yourself.*
> —Fyodor Dostoevsky
> *The Brothers Karamazov*

"The first time I met Michael was at the 1986 All-Star Game in Dallas," said NBA publicist Terry Lyons. "When he got to the hotel, there was a frenzy of interview requests. I told Michael what we needed. He said, 'Let me go to my room, and I'll be down in fifteen minutes.' I thought, 'Yeah, sure.' But at the 14:59 mark, the elevator doors opened, and there

> *The day Michael reported to me in Birmingham, I said, "Michael, we don't know each other, but I'm really going to have to treat you like anyone else," Michael said, "That's fine with me." That's how our relationship started.*
> —Terry Francona
> BIRMINGHAM MANAGER, 1994

was Michael, ready to go. He shot me a look that said, 'Did you think I'd be late?'"

None of us has to do these things. We face meetings with people each day, and we are afforded a choice. We can wall ourselves off, become like the athletes who avoid the media, who berate the officials, who ignore their coaches, who shroud themselves in contentiousness.

Or we can lift ourselves above it.

"Parents could look up to Michael," Terry Pluto said, "because he wouldn't let their kids down."

Two things John Hefferon told me. It was 1996, and Hefferon was the Bulls team doctor, and the Bulls were getting ready for a play-off game against my Magic (by the way, Chicago swept the series, thank you very much).

I had asked Hefferon about Michael Jordan. His reply: "The most remarkable person I've ever known."

"Why?" I asked.

Two things, he said. The first is that Jordan had no fear of success. Certain people, Hefferon said, are afraid to succeed because they know they'll have to keep doing it, and this scares them. Not Jordan.

The second thing is that Jordan respects all people equally.

"When Michael was a young player, he would get on the refs," said former NBA official Billy Oakes. "He started on me one night and I told him, 'I have respect for you, and I expect it from you.' That changed our entire relationship."

As Jordan matured, he learned what Oakes meant. He was careful in his speech. His blowups were infrequent, and when they happened, they were usually tempered by some sort of apologetic gesture. During a play-off game against Philadelphia, Jordan drove hard to the basket, scored and turned to referee Wally Rooney, asking for the foul call. Rooney didn't call it. Jordan eyeballed him on his way downcourt, and Rooney told him to stop it; when Jordan didn't, he called a technical foul.

After the game, Jordan was still livid. He passed Rooney on the way to a postgame interview and ripped him again. But when asked by the interviewer, Doug Collins, what he'd said, Jordan showed instant respect to Rooney and told Collins, "I was just apologizing for getting the technical."

In the midst of a play-off series against Charlotte, NBA official Dick Bavetta—perhaps the league's most respected referee—whistled Jordan for a technical after they got into it about a couple of traveling calls. Jordan was quoted about the incident in the next day's edition of the *Charlotte Observer.* He said that Bavetta was right, that he was wrong, that Bavetta was in charge of the game.

"That," Bavetta said, "was the kind of respect that Michael Jordan showed for the refs."

He cultivated relationships with the officials, as he did with the media. Once, after a Christmas day game, he saw referee Scott Foster walk past, and in the midst of a press conference, called out, "Hey, Scott, Merry Christmas."

"I didn't even know Michael Jordan knew my name," Foster said.

*Respect builds trust. Trust builds loyalty.*

Eventually, Jordan developed playful relationships with the writers and referees he knew well, so he could walk down a hallway and say, "Hey, scrub," to a reporter he knew, so he could tease the referees during a game, so he could speak to them honestly. Some would say that Jordan got away with things because of this. His penchant for avoiding traveling calls has been explored extensively. Said former official Jack Madden: "Michael got away with a lot of walking violations. I'd call it on him, but I was in the minority. He hated to see me come referee." And perhaps he did get away with more, and perhaps he didn't. But if nothing else, he had a sense of humor about it.

One night in Chicago, Paul Mihalik was officiating when Jordan made a steal, dribbled downcourt, took off at around the free-throw line, did a 360-degree turn and finished with a slam dunk—except the ball ricocheted off the iron and flew into the stands.

Jordan ran back upcourt with a smirk on his face. He turned to Mihalik and said, "Paul, why didn't you call traveling?"

## "We'll Get You a Ring"

*Trust men and they will be true to you. Treat them greatly, and they will show themselves great.*

—Ralph Waldo Emerson

He distributed his own tickets. He would pull out a list of names and match the names with each of the tickets with each of the seats. It was something that could have been done by a public-relations staff, by a personal assistant, by an intern, by anyone but him. But Jordan didn't see it like that. "If someone has a problem with tickets," he said, "I want them to know that I chose the location."

He gave away his kindness, his respect, his trust. All he demanded in return were the same things.

"With me, once you feel like you can't trust a person you once trusted, it's over forever," Jordan said. "I'm a person who keeps my word. I expect it from others as well."

An Orlando television broadcaster, Greg Warmoth, once showed up after a Bulls shootaround. He found Jordan in the parking lot. He asked for an interview and Jordan declined. Later, a Bulls' public-relations official said, "When MJ comes in the building, he's on the clock. When he leaves, he's off it."

"In effect," Warmoth said, "Michael said to me, 'You're late, and that's not professional.'"

*Respect builds trust. Trust builds loyalty.*

"Michael Jordan could have circumvented the rules of life because of his talent," said *Sports Illustrated* photographer Walter Iooss. "But when he made a commitment to do something, he always followed through."

He expected the same from his teammates. They

had to earn his trust. Once they'd come through, he'd do anything for them.

"One year Michael won the slam-dunk contest and got a check for twelve thousand dollars," said his former teammate, Elston Turner. "Next day, I walked into the training room and there was Michael, sitting at a table, writing each of us a personal check for one thousand dollars."

He promised a championship ring to Bobby Hansen, the twelfth man on the Bulls roster in 1992. Hansen came to the Bulls in a trade with Sacramento. the first time Jordan saw him, he looked at his shoes.

"You can't wear those," Jordan said.

The next day, there were a dozen pairs of Nikes waiting in Hansen's locker.

"My first game was at Boston," Hansen said. "When I got in, MJ penetrated and kicked the ball out to me. I was wide open and Michael gave me that look, like 'You'd better not miss this.' I hit the shot. He was the happiest guy in the building."

Hansen didn't see much playing time, but every time Jordan saw he was down, he'd walk over to him and say, "You hang in there. We'll get you a ring."

And they did. The Bulls beat Portland in the NBA Finals in 1992. The subs—Hansen among them—helped rally the Bulls from a fifteen-point fourth-quarter deficit in the last game. When it was over, Hansen chased down the game ball. He brought it to Jordan and said, "Do you want this?"

Jordan took it. It was a small token, a gesture of trust between teammates, between friends.

# It's That Simple

*Loyalty means not that I agree with everything you say, or that I believe you are always right. Loyalty means that I share a common ideal with you and, regardless of minor differences, we strive for it, shoulder to shoulder, confident in one another's good faith, trust, constancy and affection.*

—Dr. Karl Menninger

It is important to emphasize the rarity of the relationship between Jordan and Phil Jackson. When the Bulls signed Jackson to a one-year contract extension in 1997 after Jordan declared that he would not come back if Jackson did not come back, it defied every norm in a league in which the players dictate so much, in which it is not uncommon for players to form a mutiny to get rid of their coach.

As the lines of tension between Bulls players and coaches and management grew taut, here was Jordan, the preeminent athlete of his time, taking a stand for his coach. Declaring, "I won't play. I'll retire. It is that simple. I won't play for another coach. I will totally retire. That clears up every question. If management is saying that Phil is out, then this is my last year."

> When I was with the Spurs one night in Chicago, I was lighting up on Ron Harper pretty good. Harper couldn't check me, so he started trashing me, trying to throw me off my game. I went back at him, too. Later, at the other end, MJ walked past me and slugged me right in the stomach. I mean, he really popped me. He was saying, in effect, "Don't mess with my teammates. You mess with them, you deal with me, too."
> —Monty Williams
> NBA PLAYER

Say what you will about the egos involved, about the politics involved, about the intricacies of heated negotiations and contract talks between Jackson and Bulls general manager Jerry Krause and owner Jerry Reinsdorf. Jordan's defiance stood for something more relevant than numbers; it was based on a sense of loyalty rooted in his childhood, a feeling toward his parents that led him to look in the stands before every game and locate where they were sitting.

"I'm a very loyal guy in a sense," Jordan said. "I go to battle with very few people and I can't see going into

> *When we are debating an issue, loyalty means giving me your honest opinion, whether you think I'll like it or not. Disagreement, at this stage, stimulates me. But once a decision has been made, the debate ends. From that point on, loyalty means executing the decision as if it were your own.*
> —General Colin Powell

the trenches with someone who I haven't gone through the whole process with."

Michael didn't forget people. He didn't lose his allegiances. He didn't have to, but he took a stand for the players' side during the NBA lockout.

When he saw a few of his Barons teammates two years after they'd played together, on his way to the Bulls' team bus after a game, he recognized them immediately. He asked about their families. He spent five minutes reminiscing with them. "Michael was so loyal," said Chris Collins, the son of Jordan's ex-coach, Doug Collins. "The day I signed to play college basketball at Duke (the archrival of Jordan's alma mater, North Carolina), he gave me a big punch in the chest and said, 'Now that you're a rookie, I can't talk to you anymore.' He was kidding, but he loved Carolina."

"When Michael's your friend, he's your friend," said major-league baseball player B. J. Surhoff. "He's loyal beyond loyal."

He still treats his college coach, Dean Smith, with the same reverence. Twenty years after Roy Williams first recruited him at North Carolina, Jordan still calls Williams "coach." When one of his childhood heroes, David Thompson, would do pregame clinics for the Charlotte Hornets, Jordan would tell the kids, "David Thompson was the one I looked up to when I was your age."

"I'm like a big brother to Michael," said NBA Hall-of-Famer Julius Erving. "He treats all of us older guys with respect. He's never forgotten that we'd paved the way for his generation."

So here, then, is a more rounded portrait of the man. He could be stubborn and he could be forceful, but beneath the layers of fame and competitiveness and determination, there was humanity and there was dignity. If there wasn't, this whole thing wouldn't have worked. Jordan would have stumbled, would have been tripped up by the magnitude of his own fame. "Take away all of Michael Jordan's glitz and glamour," said Bob Costas, "and you'll find that he is 100 percent genuine like no

> *In my mind, loyalty is the greatest virtue. It's the emotional glue that keeps organizations from crumbling; that keeps employees on board during tough times; that keeps customers on your side when competitors try to lure them away. It's a virtue that reveals itself in small ways more often than it does in grand dramatic gestures.*
> —Mark McCormack
> SPORTS EXECUTIVE

other athlete who has ever played any sport."

*Respect builds trust. Trust builds loyalty.*

Michael understood the equation, that the sum of the equation was what yielded his own brand of social genius. He will be remembered most prominently for the grand brush strokes of a master on the basketball court. But it is in small ways, in moments of genuine compassion, of whimsy, of kindness, in moments between man and child, between man and man, that his legacy will continue to expand.

# CHAPTER ELEVEN

# THE RIGHT CALL

**JORDAN ON CHARACTER:**

You find there is only one person who can define success in your life—and that's you.

 **A**nd so all that Michael Jordan has been taught, and all that Michael Jordan can teach us, can be brought together in a single reflection of his character during a parking lot encounter on the campus of the University of North Carolina. One afternoon, long after he had become a star, Jordan was driving his Mercedes through the North Carolina campus, on his way to watch an exhibition basketball game. And the spots in the parking lot were full.

"Park over there," said Jordan's friend Fred Whitfield, who was in the car with him. He pointed to a handicapped space.

"No way," Jordan said.

He gave two reasons why he wouldn't. First, he said someone might need it. Second, Coach Smith would kill him if he found out.

"I wouldn't be able to face him," Jordan said.

This book offers a great many positive stories about Michael Jordan. But let's make this clear: We are not proposing that Michael Jordan is without flaw, or that he is immune to failure. We are not saying that his every action is to be emulated, or that he should be deified in the way that America so often treats its heroes.

All we are saying is that Michael Jordan is a man who, despite those flaws, despite those failures, has earned his reputation. He's a man who, in the face of extreme scrutiny, has formed a distinct character that is worth preserving. It is the product of upbringing, of Jordan's parents, of his coaches, of the decisions he made to listen to and emulate those who came before him—those who set the type of example that breeds character. In turn, Jordan himself became a model. "He set the standard for superstar conduct, period," wrote Rick Telander in *ESPN* magazine.

Cotton Fitzsimmons, the veteran NBA coach, once had breakfast with Jordan's parents, and at one point Fitzsimmons said to Jordan's mother, Deloris, "I hope he never changes."

"As long as I am breathing," Deloris Jordan replied, "he will not change."

Bucky Waters, former college coach recalls a conversation he had with Deloris.

"Michael's mother once told me that the summer

he was twelve she said, 'Michael, we're packing a lunch every day and you're going to the Y to play in their basketball program.' Michael protested vehemently and said, 'Mother, I'm a baseball player. That's my sport. I'm no good at basketball.' She said, 'Well, this summer you're a basketball player because

> *Make your commitments to enduring values and institutions — honesty, integrity, trust, confidence, family and other matters of the heart. Go ahead and challenge the status quo, but you must also decide what lasts, what really counts, what no one can take away from you. These are your values, and they will accompany you wherever you work and wherever you live.*
>
> —Jack Rehm
> AUTHOR

you're not going to be roaming around the city getting in to trouble.' 'Four years later,' Deloris said, 'we were getting calls from Dean Smith and others. We had no idea that this was going to happen with Michael. How could we have ever seen it coming?'"

"Michael's dad had the same temperament as Michael," said sports scientist Jonathan Neidnagel. "They were both highly reflective and intense men. They had all this stored-up energy that they saved to use on their passions. That's why they were so competitive. They were here-and-now guys, not big-picture people. Michael's mother was totally opposite. She was more outgoing and communicative, more creative and more structured—very personable, very gracious. Michael had the ideal blending of his parents' characteristics. It was a perfect human design."

"I concentrated on teaching him values—the values any family would teach their kid," said Jordan's late father, James. "Michael was a good learner. We tried to teach him to be himself. Always like people. Never put yourself above anybody, but never put yourself below anybody. Always look at people eye to eye."

> *Values inform our conscience which influences our behavior. Our behaviors determine the quality of our lives and the meaningfulness of our personal contribution to others, to life and to history.*
> —Dr. Laura Schlessinger
> AUTHOR

Character is the sum of a man's parts. It is a product of balance in one's life, of the self-discipline to choose the correct option even when it may be the less attractive option. It is a product of faith in a standard of morals and values that one adheres to no matter the circumstances. It is the sum of all the qualities we have explored up to this point.

We will take one more trip through now, with Jordan's life and words as our guide.

# Class and Values

*Executives spend too much time drafting, wordsmithing and redrafting vision statements, mission statements, values statements, purpose statements, aspiration statements and so on. They spend nowhere near enough time trying to align their organizations with the values and visions already in place.*

—Jim Collins
*business writer*

"I don't believe in 'if,'" Jordan said. "I think there has always been a plan for my life and that I don't have any control over it. Everything that happens was determined in advance. . . . I read the Bible a lot. I see that whatever happens, happens for a reason."

"If you were to create a media athlete and star for the age of TV sports, spec-

> *You can tell the value of a man by the way he treats his wife, by the way he treats his subordinates and by the way he treats someone who can do nothing for him.*
>
> —Ken Babcock
> SPEAKER

tacular talent, mid size, well-spoken, attractive, accessible, old-time values, wholesome, clean, natural, not too good, with a little bit of devil in him, you'd come up with Michael Jordan," said his agent, David Falk.

"He's a classic example in marketing of what we call 'synergy.' The whole is much bigger than the sum of the parts."

# Honesty and Integrity

"One man cannot do right in one department of life whilst he is occupied in doing wrong in any other department," said Mahandas Mahatma Gandhi. "Life is one indivisible whole." That's what Zig Ziglar meant when he wrote, "Remember, your life is all connected."

"I could have easily lied," said Jordan, discussing whether he'd actually eaten Wheaties before signing an endorsement contract with the cereal. "But I thought, why lie? So I told them the truth. I told them that I had never eaten Wheaties and that I didn't know whether I'd even like Wheaties. I mean, we used to eat some kind of wheat puffs when I was growing up. They came in a huge bag. I don't even know if they had a brand name. We had five kids in the family. We couldn't afford Wheaties."

> *Guard your integrity as a sacred thing. Nothing is at last sacred but the integrity of your own mind.*
> —Ralph Waldo Emerson

When Jordan was at North Carolina, Doug Moe's son David played at tiny Catawba College, also in North Carolina. The net-

> *I always tell the truth the first time and do not need a good memory to remember that.*
>
> —Sam Rayburn
> FORMER SPEAKER OF THE HOUSE

work of college basketball across the state was rife with rumor; if anybody at one of the big schools had a weakness of character, it trickled down to the other programs.

"David told me that MJ was as clean as whistle," said Moe, a longtime NBA coach. "That was his reputation. I never forgot it."

In 1993, the Bulls lost a triple-overtime NBA Finals game against Phoenix. Three times during that game, Jordan told referee Darrell Garretson that his elbow was tipped while he was taking a shot and that a foul should have been called. Garretson assured Jordan he was wrong.

> *It takes twenty years to build a reputation and five minutes to ruin it. If you think about that, you'll do things differently.*
>
> —Warren Buffett

Later, Garretson watched a tape of the game. He cued those three plays. On each one, Jordan's elbow had been tipped.

"Michael," Garretson said, "was the most honest player ever."

He never asked to renegotiate a contract. For a large

part of his career, he wasn't even one of the league's highest-paid players.

"I've taught my kids to be honest and keep their word," Jordan said. "What kind of example would I be setting if I went back on mine?"

> *Glass, china and reputation are easily cracked, and never mended well.*
> —Benjamin Franklin

This was on a Sunday, during a nationally televised game between the Bulls and Magic. At the end of the first half, Jordan drove to the basket and was converged upon by two defenders; he landed in the first row of seats. The shot went in, and Jordan emerged from the mess with a gash on his forehead, but the veteran referee, Ed Rush, did not call a foul. Jordan was upset. Phil Jackson stormed onto the floor and Rush whistled him for a technical.

As the half ended, Jordan approached Rush and said, "Look at the tape. You'll see the foul."

Rush checked the tape. There was no foul. Jordan's athleticism had allowed him to avoid the contact.

At the beginning of the second half, Rush gave Jordan a hard stare. "There was no foul on that play," he said.

"You're right," Jordan said. "It was the right call."

"Go tell that to Phil," Rush said.

So Jordan went to Jackson and told him there was no foul.

"There has to be a sense of trust between the player and referee," said Rush, "and Michael always had that."

"Michael is a man of his word," said former college coach George Raveling. "If he tells you he'll meet you at 9 A.M., you can set your watch by it."

Sean Hill was fifteen years old during the 1986–87 season, and was working as a bus boy at Pinehurst Country Club, a renowned golf resort in North Carolina. He was also a Celtics fan, and so when Jordan came to play golf there one afternoon, Hill and his friend began to taunt Jordan, telling him he wouldn't even score twenty points the next time he faced Boston. They wound up betting five dollars on it.

The next time MJ played Boston, he was

> *There are no minor lapses of integrity.*
> —Tom Peters
> SPEAKER/AUTHOR

hurt and only played half the game. He failed to score twenty. A week after the game, an envelope came for Hill, with no notes, no photos—nothing except a five-dollar check from Michael Jordan.

"My buddy still has it in a frame," Hill said.

In 1995 Michael put together a company to install driving ranges in various cities to teach golf to inner city children. Orlando businessman Jim English and his friend Gary Sorensen invested $35,000 a piece in two limited units. Two years later the venture failed and was sold. Michael agreed to consult with the acquiring company in order to get the price high enough to ensure that all investors would receive 100 percent of their money back. This included all the investors except Michael and another man who lost what they put up. Said English, "Michael ranks up there with the best, a man of integrity."

# Maturity

*Emotional maturity is one of the most important and respected qualities of leadership. It requires, first, that you are at peace with yourself and, second, that you remain calm in the face of adversity and difficulty.*

—Brian Tracy
*speaker and author*

There was a time, not long ago, when sixteen of my children were teenagers at the same time. (Somehow, I am still here.) Needless to say, the buzzword around our house at that time was maturity. As in, "Dad, I've been very mature lately. Can I borrow the car tonight?" Or, "Dad, I'm so mature, I'd like to stay out late tonight." I'm still not sure exactly how to characterize

> *Maturity begins to grow when you can sense your concern for others out-weighing your concern for yourself.*
> —John MacNaughton
> AUTHOR

maturity. But my close friend, Jay Strack, has come up with as good a definition as I've heard: "When the little boy or little girl has decided to sit down permanently, and the young man or young woman has decided to stand up permanently—that's a pretty good sign that there's some maturity taking place."

> *I tell my son, "Grow up to be a man. It's a waste of time and life to grow up to be a boy."*
> —Leonard Pitts Jr.
> NEWSPAPER COLUMNIST

Here are the six basic principles of maturity, courtesy of authors Mortimer J. Feinberg and John J. Tarrant:

1. Accept yourself
2. Accept others
3. Keep your sense of humor
4. Appreciate simple pleasures
5. Enjoy the present
6. Welcome work

"When I was at Maryland, I recruited MJ," said NBA veteran Buck Williams. "He had a lot of character, even at seventeen. He was really mature. He had a great

> *A sign of maturity is accepting deferred gratification.*
> —Adlai Stevenson

idea of what he wanted to do with his life."

"Michael looked like a champion and acted like one," said Hall of Fame coach Red Auerbach. "He was always a model. He dressed like a winner. He always had control of himself. He always said the right thing."

Mitch Albom, a Detroit sport columnist, saw an example of Jordan's maturity and sportsmanship in 1991. "The Bulls swept the Pistons out of the play-offs in a 4–0 series, thus ending three straight years of frustrating losses to Detroit. As the fourth game in 1991 was ending, all of the Pistons left the floor and never even shook hands with the Bulls, except for Joe Dumars and John Salley. MJ never said a word about that—never commented. He just ignored the Pistons' actions because he knew the Bulls had paid their dues and their time was coming. Michael refused to sink to the Pistons' level of poor sportsmanship."

> *Emotional maturity is a preface for a sense of values. The immature person exaggerates what is not important. Maturity begins when we're content to feel we're right about something without feeling the necessity to prove someone else wrong.*
> —Vince Lombardi

# Patience

*Patience is the most necessary quality for business. Many a man would rather you heard his story than grant his request.*

—Lord Chesterfield
*author and statesman*

During spring training 1994, Jordan was playing in an exhibition game with the White Sox. He'd gone zero for his last nineteen, and late in the game he chopped a ball down the third-base line and beat it out for a hit. The players had a small celebration for him after the game, and Frank Thomas came up to Jordan at his locker and said, "Are you proud of yourself?"

> *On the whole, it is patience which makes the final difference between those who succeed or fail in all things. All the greatest people have it in an infinite degree and, among the less, the patient, weak ones always conquer the impatient, strong.*
>
> —John Ruskin
> BUSINESS EXPERT

"Yes," Jordan said, "I am."

This one's about me. I flew from Orlando to Detroit to give a speech to Ford Motor Company a few years ago. A limo driver was supposed to meet me at the baggage area, but he never showed. It took about an hour, but I found another ride to the hotel, where a trainee at the front desk took his time checking me in. I paced. I sighed. I fidgeted.

And then the man in front of me in line exploded. He said I was impatient. He said I had a bad attitude. He was right, of course, and the only thing I could hope was that he wouldn't be at my speech the next day.

Next morning, in the elevator on the way to my speech, there he was. Turned out he was employed by a company that improved hotel efficiency, and he was working on a way for guests to pick up a key and go right to their rooms without checking in.

I was thoroughly humbled.

# Humility

*Keep in mind that there are laws independent of man's consent, ruling over reality, over nature, over man, too, whether is willing to recognize them or not . . . to which we must bow, unless we think we can rule ourselves, independently of the rest of nature. Egoism, in other words, must be defeated in self. The egoist is never happy.*

—Vince Lombardi

There is still debate whether this is a true event or a legend that took place in Atlantic City, New Jersey, but it's one of my favorite Jordan stories. A woman broke away from a slot machine to take a bucketful of quarters to her room before returning for dinner. She called the elevator. On it were two men. Two black men. One was extraordinarily tall. The woman hesitated before getting on the elevator.

*They're going to rob me,* she thought.

*Don't be a bigot,* she told herself.

She got in and faced the elevator doors as they closed. She waited. The elevator didn't move. Her palms were sweating. Her face was flushed.

"Hit the floor," one of the men said.

The woman threw out her arms. The bucket of quarters soared into the air and rained down upon her as she sunk.

A few seconds passed.

"Ma'am," said one of the men. "If you just tell us what floor you're going to, we'll push the button."

She turned. One of the men, the smaller one, helped her up. He was trying desperately to restrain a laugh. He bit his lip. He said, "When I told my man here to hit the floor, I meant that he should hit the elevator button for our floor. I didn't mean for you to hit the floor, ma'am."

The three of them gathered up the quarters and refilled her bucket. When the elevator arrived at her floor, the woman was still unsteady on her feet, and the men insisted upon walking her to her room.

The woman closed the door. She could hear them laughing outside.

The next day, a dozen roses arrived at her door, a one-hundred-dollar bill attached to each one.

"Thanks for the best laugh we've had in years," the card read.

It was signed by Eddie Murphy and Michael Jordan.

> *One of the things that I remember on my father's desk when he was superintendent of churches in the state was a caricature of a guy with a balloon head, string attached to the shoulders, little teensy feet. The caption on it read, "The bigger your head gets, the easier your shoes are to fill." That, to me, personified my father, who was a very humble, very approachable man. That's who I tried to emulate growing up.*
> —Phil Jackson

"People have this picture of me taking limousines, living at ... how would you say it ... at the upper echelon of life," Jordan said. "But I'm just a guy. It's funny that that's the hardest thing for people to accept. I'm just a guy who's out there having a great time playing a game."

In 1994 when Michael was just a struggling baseball player in Birmingham, he made a very revealing statement: "I'm just another minor-leaguer in the clubhouse here, trying to make it to the major leagues. You come to realize that you're no better than the next guy here."

Mark Ratenkin was a pitcher in the Arizona

> *At Michael's summer basketball camp, the sharpest kid there is Michael's son, Jeffrey. He could be the biggest jerk in the world, but he's not. He's a kind, humble young man who shows respect and consideration for everyone.*
>
> —Jimmy Williams
> CAMP COUNSELOR

Instructional League in 1994, when Jordan was playing. He struck out Jordan twice in one game. The next day, Ratenkin wanted to get Jordan's autograph, but was afraid to approach him. Eventually, he did.

Jordan signed three balls for him.

"Those were two great pitches you threw last night," Jordan said.

"I noticed a humility in Michael when he came back from baseball," said former teammate Will Perdue. "He couldn't master that game and he was different when he came back, more understanding. He saw people as they were, not as what he wanted them to be."

"One summer, Michael went back to North Carolina," said sportswriter Bill Lyon. "A little girl asked him, 'Is it true you can fly?' Michael said, 'Yes. But only for a little while.'"

"If I ask myself, 'Why me and not other people?' I'll

never come up with an answer," Jordan said. "Whatever happened to me, I didn't know it was out there. I stumbled on it and it happened. To this day, I don't know why."

Former NBA center Sam Bowie said to Michael after he made an unbelievable shot, "How did you do that?" Jordan replied. "I really don't know."

# Compassion

*No one is useless in this world who lightens the burden of it to anyone else.*
                                                —Charles Dickens

"One night, a badly burned boy sat on our bench, and Michael talked with him all night during the game," said John Bach, the former Bulls assistant coach. "I couldn't stop crying, it was so touching."

"It always touched me, the way he handled himself with the Make-A-Wish kids," said former Bulls trainer Chip Schaeffer. "He would have been a great special education teacher."

Former Bulls teammate Ricky Blanton said, "I was the ultimate NBA journeyman, but Michael treated me like I was someone special."

In 1992 JoJo English was a rookie in the Bulls' training camp, struggling through his first few days. Michael said to him, "It's not as easy as it looks on TV, is it?" From that point on he took an interest in

> *Life is a place of service. Joy can be real only if people look upon their life as a service, and have a definite object in life outside themselves and their personal happiness.*
> —Leo Tolstoy
> AUTHOR

the rookie and he helped him on and off the court. Sam Bowie said, "We all know the fifty-point side of Michael, but the human side is even better. When I was sitting on the bench with leg injuries, he never failed to come over and ask me how I was doing. He genuinely cared."

When the Bulls won a championship, Jordan spent more than six figures of his own money to have rings and pendants made up for everyone associated with the Bulls. He considered them his friends, and his friends were a crucial part of his life. His friends grounded him.

"People don't realize how important friendships were to this guy," said Jordan's personal assistant, George Koehler.

"I don't believe in race," Jordan said. "I believe in friendship."

"When I failed the bar exam for the first time, MJ gave me a pep talk," said his friend, Fred Whitfield. "He said it would be a good test of my character."

Jimmy Walker, one of Michael's financial advisors, said, "When Walter Davis had his drug problems in the mid-1980s, Michael went way out of his way to help out an old friend."

What it comes down to, then, is a shrug. It was against Portland in 1992, in Game One of the NBA Finals when Jordan couldn't seem to miss, when he wound up with thirty-five points in the first half. After sinking another three-pointer, Jordan turned to Magic Johnson, who was broadcasting the game and smiled sheepishly, turned up his hands and gave us a tiny shrug that said so much.

What the shrug told us is that Jordan doesn't understand this any better than we do. He was given an immense gift. And all he could do with it, through all of the highs and lows, was continue to be himself.

# EPILOGUE

*Dreams are what everything is about.*

—Michael Jordan

I waited until the end to speak to Ahmad Rashad. By then, the rumors about a Jordan comeback had surfaced. Writer Michael Leahy's piece in a February 2001 issue of the *Washington Post Magazine* painted Jordan as a man with a desperate competitive itch. Rick Reilly wrote a column in the March 13, 2001 issue of *Sports Illustrated* that quoted a source close to Jordan as saying he was "90 percent committed" to coming back. A media frenzy followed.

I met with Rashad—the NBC broadcaster, ex-NFL wide receiver and one of Michael Jordan's closest friends—at a Magic–Lakers game that same March. I told him the title of the book. And this is what he said:

"You can be like Mike. In fact, anyone can be like Mike."

Rashad spoke about Jordan's dedication, about his lifelong yearning to learn, to improve. He told me that Jordan set higher standards each time he tried something. He told me that Jordan was "a regular country boy who worked for everything he got."

"Being like Mike," he said, "is being successful. You set your own standard and then go after it. Set a realistic goal and then work hard. Whatever your field, you can do it. MJ is a normal guy. He just works harder than anyone else. Nothing MJ did ever shocked me or shocked him. He worked so hard, he had the confidence to do anything. Anyone can do that."

The confidence to do anything, Rashad said. Which means it would be no shock if, by the time you read this, Michael Jordan is playing basketball again. His goals, his dreams, simply won't let go. They are everything. They are the reason Michael Jordan exists.

All right, class, it's pop quiz time. Who said, "I took a cooking class when I was younger; girls weren't interested in me, and I thought, 'I may be alone for the rest of my life.'"?

If you answered "Michael Jordan" give yourself an A+.

You see, Michael Jordan, unbelievable as it may

seem, did not always exude confidence. He did, however, as we have witnessed, discover his passion—
basketball—and having fully embraced that passion,
set himself to work. But, the burden of MJ's work was
lightened because he was in love with what he was
doing.

With the work came
success, and with the
fruits of success came
more work, and with
more work came bounti-
ful          results—multiple
MVPs,     championships,
and worldwide respect.

> *There is something in
> everything I do that makes
> me dissatisfied and chal-
> lenges me to further effort.
> Sometimes, I rise above my
> level. Sometimes, I fall
> below it. But I always fall
> short of the things I never
> dream.*
>
> —H. G. Wells
> WRITER

Don't miss this point:
The passion-plus-work formula is not restricted to the
exclusive use of one Michael Jordan. It works for us. I
guarantee it!

After a speaking engagement in Minneapolis a few
years ago, I was driven to the airport by a man who had
a thirteen-year-old son. He said, "Mr. Williams, I have a
problem."

I said, "Sir, what is it?"

He related to me that his eighth-grade son loves
basketball, but wanted the assurance that he would
be granted a full scholarship to the University of

Minnesota, so that he won't invest hours and hours of hard work and practice for nothing.

I was quietly stunned. After a pregnant pause I said, "Well, sir, I'm sorry, it just doesn't work that way. Universities don't go around offering scholarships to unproven talents who are still in the eighth grade."

When I returned to Orlando, still dazed by this exchange, I asked my seventeen-year-old daughter Karyn, if this is an example of what her generation is thinking.

> *The successes I had didn't surprise me because I'd already experienced them in my mind.*
> —Michael Jordan

She replied, "Dad, I hate to tell you this, but a lot of kids my age think that way."

The point here, of course, is that there is no elevator button to push when it comes to the ladder of success, and that you don't climb that ladder with your hands in your pockets. Indeed, the only place where *success* comes before *work* is in the dictionary!

"Michael is quite free talking about his dreams, while most of us fear doing that," said writer Michael Leahy. "Michael has a unique ability to visualize his life. It's a prelude to reality. These images he has are about to be realized in his mind, and he dares to talk about them, unlike the rest of us."

In 2000, Deloris Jordan, Michael's mother, wrote a children's book about her son, called *Salt in His Shoes: Michael Jordan in Pursuit of a Dream*. It is a wonderful little book with lavish color illustrations, and a simple story that traces the same path of every successful dream. It begins with a young Jordan lamenting his size, wishing he could compete against the tallest boy on the basketball court.

"Salt," his mother says.

"Salt?" Jordan asks.

His mother tells him that she'll sprinkle salt in his shoes every night. This, she says, will help him grow. The young Jordan ponders this, then looks out the window, sees his mother's blossoming rose bushes, and realizes that perhaps his mother knows more than he does about making things grow.

And so Michael follows his mother's instructions. It is the path to every dream, the path that all of us must follow if we hope to "be like Mike."

### 1. Commit to your dream.

*In 1999, when Doc Rivers became head coach of the Magic, he FedExed a letter to all of his players. All it asked was: "Are you committed?"*

## 2. Discipline yourself.

*"Some people have greatness thrust upon them," said writer John Gardner. "Very few have excellence thrust upon them. They achieve it. They do not achieve it unwittingly, by 'doing what comes naturally,' and they don't stumble into it in the course of amusing themselves. All excellence involves discipline and tenacity of purpose."*

## 3. Risk failure.

*"The only cats worth anything are the cats that take chances," said jazz pianist Thelonious Monk. "Sometimes I play things I've never heard myself."*

## 4. Fight your fears.

*"Fear is a natural defense mechanism that sharpens your senses and your wits," said General Norman Schwarzkopf. "It's really an ally that makes you more effective at overcoming the source of your fear. There's no reason to hide your fear if it's rational. What you do need to guard against is allowing fear to paralyze you or cause you to react irrationally."*

Burning inside of Michael Jordan is a child's dream. It nags at him, it prods him, it urges him to press onward. And the dream won't allow him to relax. It won't let him settle down. He watches the best of the active players in the NBA, the hype for Allen Iverson and Kobe Bryant and Tracy McGrady and Vince Carter, and he says to himself, "You know what? I could do that, too." Behind those glistening eyes,

> *Michael followed his dreams by setting goals, working hard, and being dedicated. It's only when we do this that our dreams can and do come true.*
> —Deloris Jordan

those sleek lines, that bald head, that pigeon-toed walk, there is a man who played through sickness, who played through pain, who played through double- and triple-teams, who played with the game on the line and season on the line and history on the line.

And always, he will wonder: *What else can I do?*

Mark McCormack, sports executive, said, "The champion's true edge exists solely in the mind, and over the years I have observed three attitudinal characteristics that are common to every superstar I have ever known: The first is the champion's profound sense of dissatisfaction with his or her accomplishments. They use any success, any victory, as a spur to greater ambition. Any goal that is attained immediately becomes the next step toward a greater more "unreachable" one. The second is an ability to peak their performances to get themselves up for major tournaments or events. The legends of any sports era always seems to perform at their best when the stakes are the greatest. Finally, it is their ability to put their opponents away. This is referred to as "the killer instinct," but that tells you more about the result than of what is going on mentally. In the champion's mind he is never ahead. He distorts reality to serve his competitive purpose. He is always coming from behind, even when the score indicates he is destroying his opponent."

The greatest athletes can never relax their grip. This is why they so rarely retire gracefully. It can be a cruel fate for an athlete, but the truth is that there is no more admirable trait in a man than merely having great expectations for himself.

So I close this book as Michael Jordan ponders a comeback, as he asks himself how far he can carry *his* dream. How far will you carry *your* dream? We all have some of Michael Jordan lying dormant within us. All you have to do is release the weights that are holding you down; let go of the restraints that tie you in knots and keep you locked away from the *real* you— the you *wanting* to "be like Mike."

# AFTERWORD

## By Michael Weinreb

The other night, I began watching the tail end of a nineteen-hour Michael Jordan Marathon on ESPN Classic. I saw Michael shoot over Bryon Russell in Game Six of the 1998 NBA Finals. I saw Michael's gray pallor in Game Five of the 1997 Finals, the Sick Game. I saw Michael score thirty-five points in the first half in Game One of the 1992 Finals against Portland. I was lost. I was mesmerized. Michael toweled the sweat off his forehead. Michael shrugged his shoulders and grinned.

When I looked at the clock again, it was 4 A.M.

The weird thing was that watching it again made it all seem like it happened ages ago; it carries such historic context. "He is a slice of Americana now," as *Chicago Tribune* columnist Bob Greene notes. "He's one of those rare figures who dominated our culture. He pioneered the position. And there won't be another one."

And to think of all the time we spent chasing our own tail. The stories we wrote. The arguments we had: *The Next Michael is Grant Hill. The Next Michael is Jerry Stackhouse.* We assumed that The Next Michael was somewhere, gestating within the body of Tracy McGrady or Allen Iverson or Kobe Bryant, that he was merely waiting for the proper moment to waggle his tongue and make himself seen.

Well, as Grant Hill wrote in the introduction to this book, that's enough of that. Searching for The Next Michael is like looking for the next Enrico Caruso in a room full of lounge singers. It was a way of amusing ourselves until we came to the proper realization that the man you have just read about is not ever going to be replicated. Certainly, the next generation may show us flashes: a dizzying spin move, a dunk that leaves a lump in our throat, a blur of a crossover dribble; perhaps even a couple of NBA championship rings and the hint of a dynasty.

But The Next Michael Jordan? No. Uh-uh. Not going to happen.

I hope you have figured it out after eleven chapters, but let me repeat it: *This man is an anomaly*.

The things he has done are stunning, but the things he *is* are equally admirable. He is a leader, a champion, a role model, a father, a teammate, a golfing buddy. He is one of the few figures to transcend the skepticism of my generation, a man whom no one would dare ridicule, whom no one would dare disrespect. He rises above our natural tendency toward cynicism, appealing even to those who favor their heroes on the fringes of society (see Dennis Rodman). We see his glistening bald head, his smooth skin, his sculpted body, his tailored suits, and we carry with us a picture of a graceful man with a monumental gift, a picture of perhaps one of the last of the great American icons.

It speaks a great deal that in doing fifteen hundred interviews for this book, Pat Williams received only four negative responses. Two were from autograph seekers, a group of people who will earn absolutely no sympathy from me. Two others were from sportswriters, a notoriously grumpy bunch. You will also note that we quoted dozens of sportswriters and autograph seekers who testified to Jordan's equity with them. I challenge you to name one other celebrity who could elicit that type of response.

A radio commentator in Chicago recently referred to the head of Al Gore's legal team, David Boies, as "the

Michael Jordan of litigators." When *Washington Post* reporter Michael Leahy passed this onto Jordan, he smiled and nodded. "The standard," he said.

If anything, that's why this story needs to be passed on to the next generation. Because we read the story of Jordan and the Sick Game and we push ourselves to work through our paltry midwinter colds. Because we read the stories of Jordan and his patience with handicapped children and we think twice the next time we come across a child with Down's syndrome. Because this man is not normal. Because this man is the standard. If you get nothing else out of this book, I hope you realize that.

Lately, the question of another Jordan comeback has arisen. As I write this, I don't know what's going to happen. Nobody except Jordan seems to know. But it's funny. I have heard people say that he is too old, that he can't compete, that he can't lead his team to the play-offs, that he can't carry a team on his back anymore. And every time I have this conversation, I imagine Michael Jordan in a gym somewhere, shooting free throw after free throw, working on a new jump shot, doing sets of bicep curls until he can barely breathe, and waiting for the proper moment to emerge from history, to show himself as the only Next Michael Jordan we will ever know.

# ABOUT THE AUTHOR

Pat Williams is the senior vice president of the Orlando Magic, a franchise he cofounded in 1987. He is a veteran of thirty-three seasons in the National Basketball Association, serving as the general manager of the Chicago Bulls, Atlanta Hawks, Philadelphia 76ers and the Orlando Magic. Twenty-two of his teams have made the NBA play-offs, five have gone to the Finals, and in 1983 the Philadelphia 76ers won the NBA championship.

During his career Williams has traded Pete Maravich, traded for Julius Erving, Moses Malone and Penny Hardaway, and drafted Charles Barkley and Shaquille O'Neal.

Prior to his involvement in the NBA, Pat spent seven years in the Philadelphia Phillies organization, two years as a minor-league catcher and five in the front office. He also spent three seasons as an executive in the Minnesota Twins organization.

Williams is a 1962 graduate of Wake Forest University. He earned his master's degree from Indiana University in 1964 and was awarded an honorary doctorate from Flagler University in 1995.

Pat is one of America's top motivational speakers. He speaks more than a hundred times a year and has addressed many of the Fortune 500 companies. He has authored twenty-two books on a wide range of subjects. His much anticipated autobiography, *Ahead of the Game,* was released in 1999.

Pat and his wife Ruth are the parents of nineteen children, including fourteen who are adopted from South Korea, the Philippines, Romania and Brazil. At one point, sixteen of the children were teenagers at the same time. Two of their sons are members of the United States Marine Corps and son Bobby is a coach in the Cincinnati Reds farm system.

Pat has completed eighteen marathons in the last six years, including six consecutive Boston Marathons. He is a Sunday school teacher, a Civil War buff, a weight lifter, and a serious baseball fan. Each winter Pat catches in Major League Baseball fantasy camps and like Michael Jordan, is always considering a comeback.

If you would like to contact Pat Williams directly or if you have a Michael Jordan story you would like to share, please call him on his private line at 407-916-2404 or e-mail him at *pwilliams@rdvsports.com*. Mail can be sent to the following address:

Pat Williams

c/o RDV Sports

8701 Maitland Summit Blvd.

Orlando, FL 32810

If you would like information regarding Pat Williams's speaking engagements, please contact his assistant, Melinda Ethington. She can be reached at the above address or on her direct line at 407-916-2454. Requests can also be faxed to 407-916-2986 or e-mailed to *methington@rdvsports.com*.

# LIST OF INTERVIEWS

I would like to make it clear that I did not interview Michael Jordan for this book. All of the Jordan quotes that appear within are pieced together from various sources. I did, however, interview virtually everyone else who had ever had a conversation with Michael Jordan. At last count, this list includes fifteen hundred people including eighty of Michael's former Chicago Bulls teammates, coaches and staff, and most of his North Carolina teammates and coaches. I've heard a well-researched biography would involve between two hundred and four hundred interviews, but those who know me will vouch for the fact that I've always been given to overkill.

I did write Michael a letter of explanation as this book was being put together, and I believe I have reason to thank him. When I placed a call to his personal trainer, Tim Grover, he told me that he had an understanding with Michael: He would not talk about their relationship without Michael's permission.

Five minutes later my phone rang.

"What do you want to know?" Grover said.

So thanks to everyone on this list. And thanks, especially, to the one person who is not on this list.

# Current NBA Players

Mahmoud Abdul-Rauf
Tariq Abdul-Wahad
Shareef Abdur-Rahim
Cory Alexander
Ray Allen
John Amacchi
Derek Anderson
Kenny Anderson
Nick Anderson
Shandon Anderson
Greg Anthony
Darrell Armstrong
Ike Austin
Vin Baker
Dana Barros
Brent Barry
Jon Barry
Tony Battie
Corey Benjamin
David Benoit
Chauncey Billups
Corie Blount
Muggsy Bogues
Bruce Bowen
Shawn Bradley
Chucky Brown
Dee Brown
P.J. Brown
Randy Brown
Kobe Bryant
Mark Bryant
Jud Buechler
Matt Bullard
Scott Burrell

Jason Caffey
Marcus Camby
Elden Campbell
Chris Carr
Vince Carter
Sam Cassell
Kelvin Cato
Duane Causwell
Cedric Ceballos
Calbert Cheaney
Chris Childs
Doug Christie
Derrick Coleman
Bimbo Coles
Tyrone Corbin
Chris Crawford
John Crotty
Bill Curley
Dell Curry
Michael Curry
Erick Dampier
Antonio Daniels
Kornel David
Antonio Davis
Dale Davis
Hubert Davis
Terry Davis
Vinny Del Negro
Tony Delk
Vlade Divac
Sherman Douglas
Chris Dudley
Tim Duncan
Tyus Edney
Kevin Edwards
Howard Eisley
Mario Elie

Sean Elliott
LaPhonso Ellis
Pervis Ellison
Patrick Ewing
Jamie Feick
Danny Ferry
Michael Finley
Derek Fisher
Greg Foster
Rick Fox
Adonal Foyle
Todd Fuller
Lawrence Funderburke
Dean Garrett
Chris Gatling
Matt Geiger
Kendall Gill
Brian Grant
Gary Grant
Horace Grant
A.C. Green
Tom Gugliotta
Penny Hardaway
Tim Hardaway
Ron Harper
Othella Harrington
Lucious Harris
Antonio Harvey
Hersey Hawkins
Michael Hawkins
Alan Henderson
Cedric Henderson
Grant Hill
Tyrone Hill
Fred Hoiberg
Robert Horry
Alan Houston

Lindsey Hunter
Steven Hunter
Zydrunas Ilgauskas
Allen Iverson
Bobby Jackson
Jarren Jackson
Jimmy Jackson
Mark Jackson
Antawn Jamison
Avery Johnson
Earvin Johnson
Larry Johnson
Eddie Jones
Popeye Jones
Adam Keefe
Shawn Kemp
Steve Kerr
Jerome Kersey
Jason Kidd
Kerry Kittles
Brevin Knight
Travis Knight
Tony Kukoc
Christian Laettner
Voshon Lenard
Grant Long
Luc Longley
George Lynch
Don MacLean
Corey Maggette
Dan Majerle
Danny Manning
Stephon Marbury
Donyell Marshall
Darrick Martin
Jamal Mashburn
Anthony Mason

Tony Massenburg
Vern Maxwell
Walter McCarty
George McCloud
Antonio McDyess
Jeff McGinnis
Tracy McGrady
Jim McIlvaine
Derrick McKey
Aaron McKie
Ron Mercer
Darius Miles
Reggie Miller
Terry Mills
Sam Mitchell
Eric Montross
Alonzo Mourning
Lamond Murray
Tracy Murray
Dikembe Mutombo
Steve Nash
Johnny Newman
Moochie Norris
Charles Oakley
Hakeem Olajuwon
Jermaine O'Neal
Shaquille O'Neal
Greg Ostertag
Bo Outlaw
Doug Overton
Billy Owens
Robert Pack
Cherokee Parks
Vitaly Patapenko
Gary Payton
Will Perdue
Sam Perkins

Elliott Perry
Wes Person
Eric Piatkowski
Paul Pierce
Scottie Pippen
Scott Pollard
Olden Polynice
Mark Pope
Terry Porter
Brent Price
Laron Profit
Theo Ratliff
Eldridge Recasner
Bryant Reeves
Don Reid
J. R. Reid
Glen Rice
Quentin Richardson
Mitch Richmond
Isaiah Rider
Cliff Robinson
David Robinson
Glenn Robinson
Larry Robinson
Carlos Rogers
Rodney Rogers
Sean Rooks
Jalen Rose
Malik Rose
Byron Russell
Arvydas Sabonis
Brian Shaw
Reggie Slater
Charles Smith
Joe Smith
Michael Smith
Steve Smith

Tony Smith
Eric Snow
Felton Spencer
Latrell Sprewell
Jerry Stackhouse
John Starks
Michael Stewart
Bryant Stith
Damon Stoudamire
Erick Strickland
Mark Strickland
Rod Strickland
Derek Strong
Bob Sura
Zan Tabak
Maurice Taylor
Jamaal Tinsley
Kurt Thomas
Tim Thomas
Gary Trent
Nick Van Exel
Keith Van Horn
Jacque Vaughn
Loy Vaught
Antoine Walker
Samaki Walker
Ben Wallace
Rasheed Wallace
Charlie Ward
Clarence
   Weatherspoon
Chris Webber
David Wesley
Doug West
Chris Whitney
Aaron Williams
Alvin Williams

Eric Williams
Jerome Williams
Monty Williams
Scott Williams
Walt Williams
Corliss Williamson
Kevin Willis
Lorenzen Wright

# Former
# NBA Players

Alvan Adams
Michael Adams
Mark Aguirre
Danny Ainge
Mark Alarie
Ron Anderson
B. J. Armstrong
Keith Askins
John Bagley
Greg Ballard
Gene Banks
Charles Barkley
Rick Barry
John Battle
Elgin Baylor
Kent Benson
Otis Birdsong
Rolando Blackman
Ricky Blanton
Tom Boerwinkle
Sam Bowie
Bill Bradley
Adrian Branch
Mike Bratz

Randy Breuer
Gary Brokaw
Scott Brooks
Mike Brown
Quinn Buckner
Austin Carr
Kenny Carr
Bill Cartwright
Harvey Catchings
Rex Chapman
Maurice Cheeks
Michael Cooper
Wayne Cooper
Dave Corzine
Terry Cummings
Earl Cureton
Brad Davis
Charles Davis
Johnny Davis
Mel Davis
Walter Davis
Darryl Dawkins
Dell Demps
James Donaldson
Greg Dreiling
Larry Drew
Clyde Drexler
Mark Eaton
Franklin Edwards
James Edwards
Craig Ehlo
Dale Ellis
Len Elmore
Chris Engler
Alex English
Jojo English
Julius Erving

Michael Evans
Tony Farmer
Duane Ferrell
Eric "Sleepy" Floyd
Walt Frazier
World B. Free
George Gervin
Armon Gilliam
Artis Gilmore
Ronnie Grandison
Harvey Grant
Rickey Green
Sidney Green
David Greenwood
Darrell Griffith
Jack Haley
Tom Hammonds
Bobby Hansen
Bill Hanzlik
Derek Harper
Gerald Henderson
Carl Herrera
Rod Higgins
Roy Hinson
Craig Hodges
Michael Holton
Dennis Hopson
Jeff Hornacek
Phil Hubbard
Bobby Hurley
Dennis Johnson
Eddie Johnson
George Johnson
Kevin Johnson
Marques Johnson
Steve Johnson
Sam Jones

Clark Kellogg
Tim Kempton
Stacey King
Greg Kite
Joe Kleine
Jon Koncak
Larry Krystkowiak
Bob Lanier
Rusty Larue
Jim Les
Clifford Levingston
John Long
Bob Love
Maurice Lucas
Kyle Macy
Jeff Malone
Moses Malone
Sarunas Marciulionis
Wes Matthews
Rodney McCray
Xavier McDaniel
Kevin McHale
Billy McKinney
Dirk Minniefield
Sidney Moncrief
Chris Morris
Chris Mullin
Calvin Murphy
Pete Myers
Calvin Natt
Ed Nealy
Chuck Nevitt
Norm Nixon
Jawann Oldham
Louis Orr
Robert Parish
John Paxson

Chuck Person
Jim Petersen
Eddie Pinckney
Ben Poquette
Paul Pressey
Harold Pressley
Mark Price
Kevin Pritchard
Kurt Rambis
Mark Randall
Leo Rautins
Clifford Ray
Khalid Reeves
Pooh Richardson
David Rivers
James Robinson
Lorenzo Romar
Dan Roundfield
Donald Royal
John Salley
Ralph Sampson
Jeff Sanders
Dan Schayes
Dwayne Schintzius
Detlef Schrempf
Dennis Scott
Rony Seikaly
Brad Sellers
Purvis Short
Jerry Sichting
Jack Sikma
Dickey Simpkins
Charles Smith
Doug Smith
Kenny Smith
Larry Smith
Michael Smith

Otis Smith
Rik Smits
Mike Smrek
Rory Sparrow
Reggie Theus
Brooks Thompson
David Thompson
LaSalle Thompson
Mychal Thompson
Bob Thornton
Darren Tillis
Wayman Tisdale
Kelly Tripucka
Trent Tucker
Elston Turner
Jeff Turner
Mel Turpin
Darnell Valentine
Norm Van Lier
Kiki Vandeweghe
Sam Vincent
Darrell Walker
Bill Walton
Spud Webb
Bill Wennington
Mark West
Ennis Wheatley
Morlon Wiley
Jamaal Wilkes
Dominique Wilkins
Gerald Wilkins
Buck Williams
Corey Williams
Herb Williams
Randy Wittman
Dave Wohl
Joe Wolff

Mike Woodson
Haywoode Workman
Tony Farmer

## NBA Head Coaches

Rick Adelman
Rick Carlisle
Doug Collins
Dave Cowens
Tim Floyd
Alvin Gentry
Phil Jackson
Lon Kruger
Sidney Lowe
Nate McMillan
Don Nelson
Jim O'Brien
Greg Popovich
Pat Riley
Doc Rivers
Flip Saunders
Byron Scott
Paul Silas
Scott Skiles
Jerry Sloan
Isaiah Thomas
Rudy Tomjanovich
Jeff Van Gundy
Lenny Wilkens

# NBA Assistant Coaches and Scouts

Ron Adams
Stan Albeck
Mitchell Anderson
Randy Ayers
John Bach
Ed Badger
Bill Berry
Bill Bertka
Marty Blake
Ryan Blake
Jim Boylan
Jim Boylen
Jim Brewer
Herb Brown
Tony Brown
Pete Carril
John Carroll
Dwayne Casey
Gordon Chiesa
Tom Cirincione
Jim Cleamons
Lester Conner
Louie Dampier
Mel Daniels
Mike D'Antoni
Hank Egan
Jim Eyen
Vern Fleming
Tim Grgurich
Frank Hamblen
John Hammond

Del Harris
Larry Harris
Dick Harter
Garfield Heard
Scott Howard
Mark Iavaroni
Brian James
Phil Johnson
Eddie Jordan
Tom Jorgensen
Yvan Kelly
John Lucas
Rick Mahorn
Brendan Malone
Mo McHone
Al Menendez
Tom Mitchell
Eric Musselman
Kenny Natt
Craig Neal
Donn Nelson
Jack Nolan
Bob Ociepka
Mark Osowski
Tree Rollins
Lee Rose
Scott Roth
Keith Smart
Erik Spoelstra
Bob Staack
Terry Stotts
Jim Strack
Mike Thibault
Tom Thibodeau
Jim Thomas
Stan Van Gundy
Bob Weinhauer

Bob Weiss
Rick Weitzman
John Wetzel
Tex Winter
Brian Winters
Hal Wissel

# Former NBA Head and Assistant Coaches

Richie Adubato
Al Attles
Red Auerbach
Butch Beard
Bernie Bickerstaff
Bill Blair
P. J. Carlesimo
M. L. Carr
Butch Carter
Fred Carter
Don Casey
Chuck Daly
Mike Dunleavy
T. R. Dunn
Bill Fitch
Cotton Fitzsimmons
Chris Ford
Mike Fratello
Matt Guokas
Leonard Hamilton
Barry Hecker
Dick Helm
Brian Hill

Lionel Hollins
George Irvine
K.C. Jones
Frank Layden
Bob "Slick" Leonard
Gene Littles
Kevin Loughery
Jim Lynam
John MacLeod
Doug Moe
Dick Motta
Kip Motta
Bill Musselman
(deceased)
Tom Nissalke
Willis Reed
Jimmy Rodgers
Ron Rothstein
Bob Salmi
Mike Sanders
Gene Shue
Dave Twardzik
Paul Westhead

# Referees
(Current and Former)

Dick Bavetta
Jim Capers
Danny Crawford
Joe Crawford
Bob Delaney
Tim Donaghy
Terry Durham
Hubert Evans
Nolan Fine

Scott Foster
Bernie Fryer
Darrell Garretson
Ron Garretson
Hue Hollins
David Jones
Lee Jones
Dee Kantner
Jess Kersey
Jim Kinsey
Jack Madden
Mike Mathis
Paul Mihalik
Jack Nies
Tommy Nunez
Ronnie Nunn
Billy Oakes
Jake O'Donnell
Violet Palmer
Blaine Reichelt
Wally Rooney
Ed Rush
Eddie F. Rush
Bill Saar
Bennett Salvatore
Earl Strom (deceased)
George Toliver
John Vanak
Leon Wood

## NBA Executives and Owners
### (Current and Former)

George Andrews
Ski Austin
Pete Babcock
Rob Babcock
Horace Balmer
Mike Bantom
Bob Bass
Dave Checketts
Bryan Colangelo
Jerry Colangelo
Dave Coskey
Pat Croce
Mark Cuban
Carroll Dawson
Ellis Dawson
Joe Dumars
Wayne Embry
John Gabriel
Ernie Grunfeld
Glen Grunwald
Sonny Hill
Billy Hunter
Stu Inman
Stu Jackson
Stan Kasten
Billy King
Billy Knight
Scott Layden
Ted Leonsis
Irwin Mandel
Jack McCloskey
Larry Miller

John Nash
Kevin O'Connor
Susan O'Malley
Joe O'Neil
Jim Paxson
Geoff Petrie
Randy Pfund
Abe Pollin
Jeff Price
Jerry Reinsdorf
Jerry Reynolds
Larry Richardson
Satch Sanders
Steve Schanwald
Carl Scheer
Norm Sonju
Jon Spoelstra
Garry St. Jean
John Steinmiller
Brendan Suhr
Rick Sund
Bill Sutton
Jack Swope
Rod Thorn
Wes Unseld
Dick Versace
Wally Walker
Chris Wallace
Jerry West
Fred Whitfield
Bob Whitsitt
Leah Wilcox
Matt Winick
Bob Zuffelato

## NBA Trainers, Doctors, Equipment Managers, and Strength and Conditioning Personnel
### (Current and Former)

Mike Abdenour
Tom Abdenour
Ted Arzonico
Walter Blase
Gary Briggs
Terry Clark
David Craig
Ron Culp
Lenny Currier
Al Domenico
Bill Foran
Tim Garl
Jim Gillen
Dr. John Hefferon
Roger Hinds
Jay Jensen
Kevin Johnson
Keith Jones
Terry Kofler
Ed Legerte
John Ligmanowski
Allen Lumpkin
Scott McCullough
Adam Nelson
Joe O'Toole
Billy Paige
Mark Pfeil

Rodney Powell
Joe Proski
Mike Saunders
Chip Schaefer
Will Sevening
Mike Shimansky
Clyde Smith
Tom Smith
Gary Vitti
Troy Wenzel

## Publicists/ Photographers

Doug Able
Dave Allred
Marty Aronoff
David Benner
Ben Bentley *(deceased)*
John Black
Joe Browning
Deborah Butt
Matt Dobek
Tim Donovan
Julie Fie
Skeeter Francis
Tim Frank
Karen Frascona
George Galante
Joel Glass
Tim Hallam
Lori Hamamoto
Jan Hubbard
Walt Iooss
Tom James
Robyn Jamilosa
Harold Kaufman

Marianne Kopini
Jim LaBumbard
Scott Leightman
Maria Ludwig
Terry Lyons
Alex Martins
Brian McIntyre
John Mertz
Craig Miller
Marc Moquin
Maureen Nasser
Harvey Pollack
Bob Price
Raymond Ridder
Bob Rosenberg
Tommy Sheppard
Bill Smith
Dan Smyczek
Mike Soltys
Kyle Spencer
Zelda Spoelstra
Kevin Sullivan
Seth Sylvan
Arthur Triche
Jeff Twiss
Matt Williams
Frank Weedon
Kent Wipf

## College Coaches
### (Head and Assistant)

Steve Alford
  University of Iowa
Tommy Amaker
  University of
  Michigan

Henry Bibby
University of
Southern California

Jim Boeheim
Syracuse University

Mike Brey
University of
Notre Dame

Jim Calhoun
University of
Connecticut

John Calipari
University of
Memphis

Chris Carlson
Northern Arizona
University (Assistant)

John Chaney
Temple University

Chris Collins
Duke University
(Assistant)

Dan Dakich
Bowling Green
State University

Johnny Dawkins
Duke University
(Assistant)

Billy Donovan
University of Florida

Lefty Driesell
Georgia State
University

Hugh Durham
Jacksonville
University

Cliff Ellis
Auburn University

Steve Fisher
San Diego State
University

Pete Gillen
University of
Virginia

Jim Harrick
University of
Georgia

David Henderson
University of
Delaware

Paul Hewitt
Georgia Tech

Bob Hill
Fordham University

Bob Huggins
University of
Cincinnati

Bobby Hussey
Clemson University
(Assistant)

Tom Izzo
Michigan State
University

Mike Jarvis
St. John's University

Jeff Jones
American University

Johnny Jones
University of
Alabama (Assistant)

Gene Keady
Purdue University

Pat Kennedy
DePaul University

Mike Krzyzewski
Duke University

Steve Lavin
UCLA

Rick Majerus
University of Utah

Phil Martelli
St. Joseph's
University

Rollie Massimino
Cleveland State
University

Mike Montgomery
Stanford University

Jim O'Brien
Ohio State
University

Dave Odom
University of
South Carolina

Lute Olson
University of
Arizona

Rick Pitino
University of
Louisville

Skip Prosser
Wake Forest
University

Jason Rabedeaux
University of
Texas El Paso

Nolan Richardson
University of
Arkansas

Steve Robinson
Florida State
University

Jeff Ruland
Iona College

Kelvin Sampson
University of
Oklahoma

Herb Sendek
North Carolina State
University

Al Skinner
Boston College

Tubby Smith
University of
Kentucky

Kirk Speraw
University of
Central Florida

Charlie Spoonhour
University of
Nevada Las Vegas

Eddie Sutton
Oklahoma State

Jerry Tarkanian
Fresno State
University

John Thompson, Jr.
Princeton
University

Monte Towe
University of
New Orleans

Paul Westphal
Pepperdine
University

Rob Wilkes
Florida State
University

Glenn Wilkes, Jr.
Rollins College

Gary Williams
University of
Maryland

# Former College Coaches

Murray Arnold

Gene Bartow

Bill Bayno

Dale Brown

Charlie Bryant

Lou Carnesecca

Bobby Cremins

Denny Crum

Don Donoher

Bill Foster

Bill Frieder

Clarence "Big House"
Gaines

Dave Gavitt

Clem Haskins

Don Haskins

Jud Heathcote

Terry Holland

John Lotz *(deceased)*

Al McGuire *(deceased)*

Joey Meyer

Ray Meyer

Pete Newell

C. M. Newton

Tom Penders

Digger Phelps

Jerry Pimm

George Raveling

Les Robinson

Wimp Sanderson

Norm Sloan

Norm Stewart

John Thompson

Bucky Waters

Glenn Wilkes

John Wooden

# University of North Carolina Basketball Family

Jimmy Black

Dudley Bradley

Rick Brewer

Larry Brown

David Chadwick

Pete Chilcutt

Geoff Crompton

Ken Crowder

Billy Cunningham

Harley Dartt

Brad Daugherty

Mark Davis

Matt Doherty

Woody Durham

Adam Fleishman

Eddie Fogler

Phil Ford

Bill Guthridge

Mia Hamm

Brendan Haywood

Curtis Hunter

Bobby Jones

George Karl

John Kuester

Mitch Kupchak

John Lacey
Angela Lee
Vicki Lotz
Warren Martin
Bob McAdoo
Mike O'Koren
Buzz Peterson
Mike Roberts
Charlie Scott
Adolph Shiver
Dean Smith
B. J. Surhoff
John Swofford
Terry Truax
Donnie Walsh
Randy Wiel
Roy Williams
Al Wood

## Michael Jordan's Baseball Associates

Mike Barnett
Curt Bloom
Peter Bragan, Jr.
Kirk Champion
Roly de Armas
Steve De Salvo
Tony Ensor
Terry Francona
Sean Gavaghan
Rubin Grant
Ken Griffey, Jr.

Bill Hardekopf
Mark Hauser
David Hersh
Gary Jones
Derek Jeter
Joe Kremer
John Kuehl
Gene Lamont
Bobby Meacham
Don Mincher
Chris Pika
Dan Rajkowski
Scott Reifert
Cal Ripken
Brian Roberts
Phil Roof
Herm Schneider
Ron Schueler
Scott Tedder
Dave Trembley
Larry Ward
Chris Weinke
Doug Wollenburg

## Sports Agents

Jeff Austin
Lon Babby
Mark Bartelstein
Norman Blass
David Bober
Frank Catapano
Bill Duffy
Tony Dutt
Todd Eley

Eric Fleisher
Marc Fleisher
Vinny Giles
Keith Glass
Sean Holley
Richard Howell
Steve Kauffman
Mark Love
Tom McLaughlin
Andy Miller
Bill Pollak
Lou Rosen
Herb Rudoy
Jimmy Sexton
Jerome Stanley
Bill Strickland
Arn Tellem
Dr. Charles Tucker
Darren Weiner

## Sportswriters and Authors

J. A. Adande
Mitch Albom
David Aldridge
Dave Anderson
Harvey Araton
Terry Armour
Geoffrey Arnold
Steve Aschburner
Lacy Banks
Barbara Barker
Skip Bayless
Howard Beck
Ira Berkow

Steve Bisheff
Fran Blineberry
Hal Bock
Hal Bodley
Greg Boeck
Rick Bonnell
Tom Boswell
Bill Brill
Chris Broussard
Tim Brown
Conrad Brunner
Ric Bucher
Steve Bulpett
Curtis Bunn
Marty Burns
Chuck Carree
George Castle
Scott Cooper
Dave D'Alessandro
Craig Daniels
Dave Del Grande
Jeff Denberg
Glenn Dickey
Kevin Ding
Nunyo Domasio
Larry Donald
   *(deceased)*
Richard Dubroff
David DuPree
John Eisenberg
Tom Emlund
Joe Falls
Perry Farrell
Bill Fay
Jonathan Feigen
John Feinstein
Lee Folger

Bob Ford
Norm Frauenheim
Tom Friend
Joe Gilmartin
Bill Gleason
Brian Golden
Ron Green, Sr.
Bob Greene
Larry Guest
Israel Gutierrez
David Halberstam
Bill Harris
Sid Hartman
Mark Heisler
Ken Hornack
Michael Hunt
Mike Imrem
Melissa Isaacson
Frank Isola
Barry Jackson
Phil Jasner
Dick Jerardi
K. C. Johnson
Tim Kawakami
Larry Keech
Steve Kelley
Omar Kelly
Milton Kent
Fred Kerber
Curry Kirkpatrick
Tony Kornheiser
Doug Krikorian
Clay Latimer
Mitch Lawrence
Leonard Laye
Roland Lazenby
Michael Leahy

David Leon Moore
Malcolm Moran
Michael Murphy
Leonard Lewin
Bernie Lincicome
Jim Litke
Bill Livingston
Johnny Ludden
Steve Luhm
Mike Lupica
Bill Lyon
Jack MacCallum
Jackie MacMullan
Jay Mariotti
Rudy Martzke
Peter May
Chris McCloskey
Kent McDill
Mike McGraw
Martin McNeal
Fred Mitchell
John Mitchell
Roman Modrowski
Mark Montieth
David Moore
Malcolm Moran
Roscoe Nance
Woody Paige
Bill Plaschke
Terry Pluto
Tim Povtak
Shaun Powell
Dwain Price
Bill Rhoden
Rick Reilly
Glenn Rogers
Barry Rozner

Bob Ryan
Jon Saraceno
Dick Scanlon
Mary Schmitt Boyer
Brian Schmitz
Dan Shaugnessy
Chris Sheridan
John Smallwood
Doug Smith
Sam Smith
Scott Soshnick
Marc Spears
Marc Stein
Matt Steinmetz
Paul Taylor
Rick Telander
Art Thiel
Ian Thomsen
Ronald Tiller
Carlton Tudor
Mike Tulumello
Brad Turner
Mark Vancil
Pete Vescey
Ailene Voisin
Brad Weinstein
Dick Weiss
Mark Whicker
Lonnie White
Michael Wilbon
Ira Winderman
Mike Wise
Steve Wyche
Bob Young
Chris Young

# Sports and News Broadcasters

Al Albert
Marv Albert
John Andariese
Scott Anez
Jim Barnett
Gary Bender
Dan Bernstein
Terry Boers
Ron Boone
Mark Boyle
Mike Breen
Hubie Brown
Lorn Brown
Steve Buckhantz
Kevin Calabro
Lou Canellis
Chip Caray
Mark Champion
Phil Chenier
Larry Conley
Chet Coppock
Bob Costas
Bob Cousy
Ted Davis
Tom Dore
Eddie Doucette
Jim Durham
Ian Eagle
Dick Enberg
Bob Fitzgerald
Jim Foley
Chris Fowler
Peter Gammons

Gary Gerould
Jack Givens
Mike Glenn
Mike Gminski
Drew Goodman
Curt Gowdy
Jim Gray
Mike Greenberg
Greg Gumbel
Deck Hardee
Ken "Hawk" Harrelson
Arne Harris
Glen Harris
Chad Hartman
Joe Hawk
Chick Hearn
Tommy Heinsohn
Rich Herrara
Steve Holman
Jay Howard
Rod Hundley
Mark Inglis
Dave Johnson
Gus Johnson
Steve Jones
David Kaplan
Jim Karvellas
Steve Kashull
Greg Kelser
Paul Kennedy
John Kerr
Albert King
Stu Lantz
Wayne Larrivee
Ralph Lawler
Bob Ley
Bob Licht

Todd Lichti
Edgar Lopez
Cedric Maxwell
Al McCoy
John McGlockin
Gil McGregor
Ann Meyers Dysdale
Cheryl Miller
Andrew Monaco
Red Mottlow
Brent Musberger
Joel Myers
Grant Napear
Bob Neal
Dennis Neumann
Bob Ortegel
Billy Packer
Jim Paschke
Dan Patrick
Gene Peterson
Matt Pinto
Nick Pinto
Don Poier
Paul Porter
Bill Raftery
Ahmad Rashad
Bob Rathbun
Cheryl Raye
Michael Rechi
Eric Reid
Dan Roan
Jim Rose
Tim Roye
Tim Russert
Greg Sacar
Dick Schaap
Jerry Schemmel

Stuart Scott
Tom Shaer
Bill Simonson
Jim Spanarkel
John St. Augustine
David Steele
Paul Sunderland
Chuck Swirsky
Joe Tait
Tom Tolbert
Jay Triano
Bob Valvano
Dick Vitale
Greg Warmoth
Bill Worrell

## Fans

Pike Abell
  Titusville, FL
Omri and Julie Amrany
  Chicago, IL
Bob Angone
  Chicago, IL
Brandon Bachner
  Chicago, IL
Dwight Bain
  Orlando, FL
Paul Berlin
  Chicago, IL
Brooks Bernard
  Lafayette, LA
James Braam
  Los Angeles, CA
Mike Bredecka
  Chicago, IL
Joe Bremnan
  Chicago, IL

Brett Buckwald
  Atlanta, GA
Ron Burger
  Chicago, IL
Tim Burton
  Rockford, IL
Wes Cantrell
  Woodstock, GA
Mark Carman
  Highland Park, IL
Elizabeth Carter
  Melbourne, FL
Lou Cella
  Chicago, IL
Jack Chapin
  Wilmette, IL
Barbara Clark
  Chicago, IL
John Collins
  Chicago, IL
Jack Cory
  Itasca, IL
Matt Davis
  Dayton, OH
Andrew Day
  Phoenix, AZ
Gary DeVroy
  Lake Bluff, IL
Marty Dim
  Deerfield, IL
Bob Donan
  Wilmette, IL
Danny Einhorn
  Phoenix, AZ
Susan Ellis
  Indianapolis, IN
Jim English
  Orlando, FL
Guadalupe Falcon
  Chicago, IL

Joseph Filippazzo
Longview, TX

Ken Frank
Joliet, IL

Jim Fuller
Chicago, IL

Fred Gamber
Chicago, IL

Stu Ganz
San Jose, CA

Ron Gerber
Orlando, FL

Daniel Getting, LA

David Glaspie
Indianapolis, IN

Diann Gordon
Carbondale, IL

Jacob Grill
Chicago, IL

Bill Gronvold, AS

Gil Gulbrandson
Chicago, IL

Franz Hanning
Orlando, FL

Mark Harada
Chicago, IL

Sean Hill
Orlando, FL

Dale Hirschfield
Chicago, IL

Pat Hogan
Chicago, IL

Michael Holecek
Chicago, IL

Bill Holmes
Sauk Village, IL

Brian Holt
Orlando, FL

Coleman Hughes
Pittsburgh, PA

Steve Hunterman
New Orleans, LA

Eric Jackson
Indianapolis, IN

Ken Jakubowski
Chicago, IL

Paul Jenista
Wilmette, IL

Tim John
Lockport, IL

Mitch Juricich
San Mateo, CA

Kelly Kaesar, CA

Jerry Kaufman
Chicago, IL

Dan Kelsey
Atlanta, GA

Lori Klingman
Chicago, IL

Aaron Kordelewski
Chicago, IL

Steve Kottler
Chicago, IL

Dan Koulianos
Chicago, IL

Jay Kreutner
New Albany, IN

Ken Kuhn
Chicago, IL

Jim Lentz
Wheaton, IL

Mike Litz
Omaha, NE

Brett McCourt
Orlando, FL

James McDonald
Chicago, IL

Vern McGonagle
Naperville, IL

Rick McHale
Fremont, CA

Terry McNutt
Melbourne, FL

Tom Miner
Phoenix, AZ

Jean Morse
Lake Forest, IL

Mark Myre
Pontiac, IL

Mark NeJame
Orlando, FL

Wengary Newton
St. Petersburg, FL

John O'Connor
San Diego, CA

Sandy Olsen
Chicago, IL

Bill Olson
Duluth, MN

Tony Opiola
Chicago, IL

Kevin Radelet
Chicago, IL

Allan Raphael
New Orleans, LA

Loren Rivkin
Chicago, IL

James Robinson
Oakland, CA

Steve Rodheim
Chicago, IL

George Sands
Torrance, CA

Dr. Ken Savage, CA

Peter Schroeder
Orlando, FL

Wally Seegren
Zion, IL

Paul Sharpe
Orlando, FL
Andy Squire
Hillside, IL
Larry Steinkamp
Chicago, IL
Harold Stork
Chenoa, IL
Jay Strack
Orlando, FL
Chad Strojinc
Chicago, IL
Lynn Sullivan
Maitland, FL
Nick Trajkovich
Naperville, IL
Cau Tran
Holland, MI
Sam Wade
Orlando, FL
Mike Wasserman
Los Gatos, CA
Rob Weber, NJ
Harvey Weinberg
Chicago, IL
Shawn White
Philadelphia, PA
Angel Wilkes
DeLand, FL
Bobby Williams
Orlando, FL
Jerome Williams
Chicago, IL
Jimmy Williams
Orlando, FL
Samuel Williams
Orlando, FL
Thomas Windon
Bacova, VA

Joy Winfrey
Orlando, FL
Ryan Wizov
Philadelphia, PA
Terrie Woznicki
Indianapolis, IN
Tim Zahr
Chicago, IL
Victor Zast
Chicago, IL
Joel Zimberoff
Chicago, IL

## Miscellaneous

Cindy Alston
Sheldon Bassett
Donna Biemiller
Jay Bilas
Warren Brown
Mark Brunnell
John Capps
Danny Chuman
Ron Coley
Joe Dean
Richard Dent
Ross Deutsch
Dick Ebersol
Chip Engelland
Justin Firestone
Tim Fox
John Fraser
Howard Garfinkel
Greg Gentile

Doc Giffin
Stedman Graham
Willie Gregory
Tim Grover
Tinker Hatfield
Chamique Holdsclaw
Ed Janka
Joe Lee
Spike Lee
Lisa Leslie
Adam Lippard
Erick Martin
Tom McGrath
Donnie Miller
Nikki McCray
Donovan McNabb
John Moores
George Mumford
Curly Neal
Richard Neher
Steve Neher
Jonathan Neidnagel
Martin Newton
Mrs. Bobby Phills
Mark Raveling
Fred Reynolds
Dave Sanford
Sonny Vaccaro
Jimmy Walker
Bill Wall
Randy Weisberg
Howard White
Tom Wiscarz

# BIBLIOGRAPHY

Beckett, Dr. James. *Michael Jordan.* Dallas: Beckett Publications, 1998.

Bird, Larry. *Bird Watching.* New York: Warner Books, 1999.

Bradley, Bill. *Values of the Game.* New York: Artisan, 1998.

Bradley, Michael. *Michael Jordan's Scrapbook.* Lincolnwood, Ill.: Publications International, Ltd., 1998.

Chadwick, David. *The 12 Leadership Principles of Dean Smith.* New York: Total/Sports Illustrated, 1999.

Chansky, Art. *Dean's Domain.* Marietta, Ga.: Longstreet, Inc., 1999.

Condor, Bob. *Michael Jordan's 50 Greatest Games.* Secaucus, N.J.: Carol Publishing Group, 1998.

Greene, Bob. *Hang Time.* New York: Doubleday, 1992.

———. *Rebound.* New York: Signet, 1996.

Halberstam, David. *Playing for Keeps.* New York: Random House, 1999.

Holdsclaw, Chamique. *Chamique: On Family, Focus, and Basketball.* New York: Scribner, 2000.

Hubbard, Jan. *Six Times As Sweet.* New York: HarperHorizon, 1998.

Jackson, Phil, and Charley Rosen. *More Than a Game.* New York: Seven Stories Press, 2001.

Jackson, Phil. *Sacred Hoops: Spiritual Lessons of a Hardwood Warrior.* New York: Hyperion, 1996.

Jeter, Derek. *The Life You Imagine.* New York: Crown Publishers, 2000.

Jordan, Deloris. *Salt in His Shoes: Michael Jordan in Pursuit of a Dream.* New York: Simon & Schuster, 2000.

Jordan, Michael. *For the Love of the Game.* New York: Crown Publishers, 1998.

Krugel, Mitchell. *Jordan: The Man, His Words, His Life.* New York: St. Martin's Press, 1994.

Lazenby, Roland. *And Now Your Chicago Bulls.* Dallas: Taylor Publishing Company, 1995.

———. *Blood on the Horns.* Lenexa, Kans.: Addax Publishing Group, Inc., 1998.

———. *Mindgames.* Chicago: Contemporary Books, 2001.

Love, Robert Earl. *The Bob Love Story.* Chicago: Contemporary Books, 2000.

Lowe, Janet. *Michael Jordan Speaks.* New York: John Wiley & Sons, Inc., 1999.

Sachare, Alex. *The Chicago Bulls Encyclopedia.* Chicago: Contemporary Books, 1999.

Smith, Dean. *A Coach's Life.* New York: Random House, 1999.

Smith, Sam. *The Jordan Rules.* New York: Simon & Schuster, 1992.

———. *The Strange Odyssey of Michael Jordan.* New York: Harper-Collins Publishers, 1995.

Vancil, Mark. *For the Love of the Game.* New York: Crown Publishers, Inc., 1998.

Wert, Jeffry D. *Gettysburg—Day Three*. New York: Simon & Schuster, 2001.

Wilkens, Lenny. *Unguarded*. New York: Simon & Schuster, 2000.

Williams, Jayson. *Loose Balls*. New York: Random House, 1999.

Winter, Tex. *Trial by Basketball*. Lenexa, Kans.: Addax Publishing Group, 2000.

# NOTES

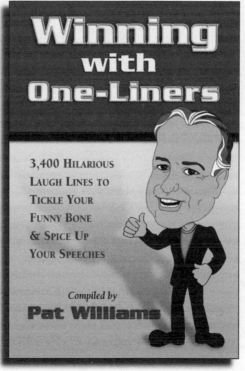

# More in the series

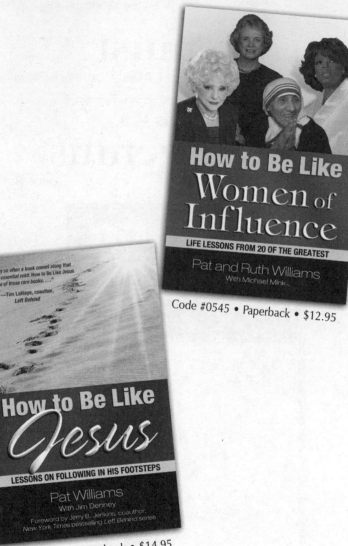

Code #0545 • Paperback • $12.95

Code #0693 • Paperback • $14.95